TEARS OF A WARRIOR

A Family's Story of Combat and Living With PTSD

www.teampursuits.com

JANET J. SEAHORN, Ph.D
E. ANTHONY SEAHORN, MBA

www.tearsofawarrior.com

Updated & Expanded
3rd EDITION − 2014

Published by
TEAM PURSUITS
3534 Harbor Way
Ft. Collins, CO 80524

Email: tseahorn@att.net or jjseahorn@att.net

www.teampursuits.com

Library of Congress Control Number: TXU001579696

ISBN: 978-0-615-21317-0

Cover design, illustrations, interior page layout by Kerrie Lian, under contract with MacGraphics Services
Cover photo credits: Author & Capt. Greg Rockwood
Editing by Karen Reddick, The Red Pen Editor

Printed in the United States of America

Forward

www.mophsf.org

The simple definition of a warrior is, "One engaged or experienced in battle" — what is not so simple to define, or describe to anyone, is each veterans individual experience within battle. Where the warrior is engaged, how each veteran participates and the physical and mental scars left over from war are all different. However, the commonality all warriors share is the experience of battle.

The Purple Heart Service Foundation in conjunction with the authors of *Tears Of A Warrior* offer this book free of charge to warriors, their families and those who work directly with warriors to help manage life after battle. We hope that by reading this book, one may find some personal control and purpose throughout the rest of their lives.

It is our hope this book will provide a starting point to those trying to understand the experience of war and is offered as a small token of admiration and respect from the Purple Heart Service Foundation to those who gave so much for our country.

God Bless the Warriors,

James M. Blaylock
President, Board of Directors
Military Order of the Purple Heart Service Foundation, Inc.
Purple Heart Recipient

Book is Provided Free to Warriors,
Their Families and Service Providers

To Reorder Book:

Phone: (703) 256-6139

Web site: www.mophsf.org

Click on PTSD BOOK

Contents

E. Anthony Seahorn   Janet J. Seahorn

This book is dedicated to the many veterans and their families; past, present and future who step forward to serve their country. We are also deeply indebted to our sons, Chad and Christopher, who endured their early years and youth trying, at times, to understand the unknowing and unexplainable behaviors of their parents. Their wisdom and courage have contributed significantly to our family's sense of unity and joy. They are a deep source of inspiration, growing into strong, contributing young men.

Preface

Tears of a Warrior: A Family's Story of Combat and Living With PTSD is a labor of deep hope and desire to make a difference for the many young men and women returning home after experiencing the trauma of combat. We began the project shortly after the start of the war in Iraq and Afghanistan. Watching the news, reading accounts of battles in the newspaper and magazines, and later hearing the stories of returning military personnel, we were reminded of the difficult journey we had faced for over thirty years.

A study done by the Department of Defense in May 2004 noted that 17-20 percent of soldiers returning from Iraq "suffer from major depression, generalized anxiety, or PTSD" according to an article by Cecilia Capuzzi Simon in *Psychotherapy Networker* (January/February 2007, 30). This percentage was influenced by the number of "firefights" the soldier had participated in and the number of tours they had served. Pauline Jelinek states in an article published May 28, 2008,

Records show roughly 40,000 troops have been diagnosed with the illness, also known as PTSD, since 2003. Officials believe that many more are likely keeping their illness a secret (www.defenselink.mil).

Paul Rieckhoff, founder of the group Iraq and Afghanistan Veterans of America, believes that PTSD is the "number one issue facing soldiers of Iraq and Afghanistan" (Paul Rieckhoff, *Psychotherapy Networker*, Simon, 31). In March 2006 the *Journal of the American Medical Association* reported that "35 percent of Iraq war veterans sought treatment for mental health issues within a year of coming home—a startling percentage, given the military's well-known resistance to therapy. Keeping in mind the percentages only reflect soldiers who admitted needing help" (31).

For years our family lived with the impact of combat Post-Traumatic Stress Disorder (PTSD) without knowing or understanding it even existed. The effects on the brain, heart, and soul are enormous, and they don't always fade away with time. The last ten years have brought us needed information regarding the specific characteristics and causes of PTSD.

Post-Traumatic Stress Disorder is the ultimate hidden enemy. It finds an individual's vulnerable spot and proceeds to terrorize that person using a variety of creative tactics. It consumes the bearer with fear, anxiety, and frustration. Never knowing when the ambush will occur, the victim is on constant alert for the next cycle of torment.

The attacks are usually unexpected and some are horrifically brutal in nature, forcing the sufferer to relive the unspeakable as if it were occurring again, and again, and again. Throbbing emotional injuries are continually reopened and resurrected from the traumatic experience, complete with agonizing feelings and poignant memories. No amount of reasoning, bargaining, or begging causes the enemy to retreat. It often returns when least expected—a reminder of a past that cannot be erased—no matter how hard one tries.

Like a ghost, PTSD sneaks into the unconscious and consumes the senses with its debilitating sights, sounds, smells, tastes, and even touches. What makes the experience so damaging is the enemy is almost impossible to clearly identify. Words can't accurately describe the culprit, for it is more emotionally influenced than consciously explained.

Many of the lessons in writing this book came from an increasing realization of our own lack of knowledge regarding Tony's Vietnam combat experience, and how trauma can impact a person. As a researcher, Jan spent countless hours reading books, articles and documents on trauma, and viewing CDs and videos of testimonials from troops returning from Iraq and Afghanistan. Their stories were frighteningly similar to ours: the nightmares, panic attacks, and need for unconditional control of almost every situation. Recalling the sleepless nights and anxiety-ridden days filled with emotional outbursts or periods of avoidance and numbness was too familiar. The depression and feelings of hopelessness was fraught with overwhelming emotional struggles. Their stories were our stories. Most of all, we did not want the new warriors and their families to have to experience a similar journey without a better roadmap than we had when Tony returned from Vietnam.

The scenarios we describe in this book take into account the numerous differences between individuals, and how each cope in their own way with the stress of combat trauma. We generally use the male gender term when discussing PTSD only because we are writing from our experiences. Yet, we are well aware that women equally experience the burdens and symptoms of combat trauma. It may be for women, the challenges of PTSD are even greater given their role of mother, nurturer, caretaker, and heart of the family. Fulfilling these roles when one's entire being is carrying the trauma of combat can be incredibly difficult. We are concerned about who will step in to nurture the nurturer. Who will protect and look after the mother? Even with the successful inclusion of women in today's military, it has also made managing family life more challenging.

While co-writing this book, Jan spent many years in the researcher mode, knowing her own coping strategy was to avoid facing the long-term emotional damage on herself and our family. Tony would begin to write his combat story, then find a number of other "more important" chores to attend to—chores that would take weeks, even months to accomplish. This was his way of avoiding the demons created as he recalled the vivid details of his combat experience. They were always present, but wore different disguises such as anger, anxiety and short temper. To possess demons is one thing, to make them more real by putting them onto paper is quite another task. In the end, Tony spent two and a half years procrastinating and ten months of incredibly intense reflection and writing. During the last months of writing, the nightmares and panic attacks increased, along with the feelings of depression and anxiety. Writing definitely had its price and it was emotionally and physically costly. However, it will have been worth the challenges and emotional angst if the information and stories in this book make a difference for even one veteran and their family.

As we write our story, it must be noted that the majority of our family life has been very loving, rich and filled with positive experiences. We have always had a deep commitment to our children and family relationship. It is that small percent of the total picture, however, that we focus on in this book. This is where the challenges of PTSD appear: unforeseen, inconsistent in appearance, and relentless in its torment. This is where the unpredictability of PTSD kept us all walking through the mine/mind field of dread. It is this "not knowing" when, where, or why, that held us somewhat hostage to an unidentified enemy. Not knowing when the next bomb might explode is the real complex part of living and dealing with PTSD. It is this part of our life that this book is about because it is this part of life that makes living with PTSD a threat to an otherwise normal family existence.

Reading Suggestions

When going through the book's contents, you do not need to read each chapter one after another, although it is important to read the Introduction and first few chapters in order to better understand the information in the other sections. The book is not meant to be read in one sitting. Take your time. Think about how the different scenarios in each chapter are similar or different than your experience. Take time to do the activities. Then take more time to read your responses, reflect on them and share them with your significant other or other supporter. Be sure to celebrate your many strengths and the fact that it took incredible courage to ride into combat, and it may take even more to survive combat's consequences after returning home. You can carry on with your life and live it fully. It helps to have a purpose greater than yourself. Find that purpose. Live it.

Other Trauma Victims

Unfortunately, trauma can affect many individuals in our society for a variety of reasons. It occurs far too often in young children due to violence, abuse, and neglect. Battered women and men suffer with its effects. Many employers, educators, health care professionals, extended family, and friends witness the symptoms of PTSD and must learn skills to acknowledge and support the sufferer. Therefore, to some extent, the content in this book is for anyone who has endured and may continue to suffer from a life-altering trauma.

We hope the book supports you and your loved ones throughout your journey. By providing you information on Post-Traumatic Stress Disorder and its emotional and physical symptoms, perhaps you will have a clearer, better roadmap to follow as you live each day. And, perhaps, your passage will be gentler, healthier and easier.

Warm regards,

Janet and Tony Seahorn

The Road Ahead   Author's Collection

Note:

Surveys and questionnaires in the book are not meant to be clinical instruments but tools for reflection that may lead the reader toward a better understanding of their personal situation. By gaining clearer insight of their past and present situation, they will be in a better position to seek additional help and support going forward.

Acknowledgments

St. Francis of Assisi stated the following: "Start by doing what's necessary, then what's possible, and suddenly you are doing the impossible." Writing this book has been much like these words of inspiration. We began the process seven years ago. We researched the topic, paying particular attention to what is happening in the brain and body when it undergoes trauma. From there we compared the information to our own experiences. Often, the process took an enormous toll on our physical and emotional being. The sleepless nights, recurrent nightmares from the memories of combat, anxiety that led over and over again to a "renewed process," plagued the journey.

At times, Tony would need to take weeks before he was able to resume writing. The pain of writing about specific events and memories were mentally exhausting, but also impacted his physical health. We didn't tell anyone, including most family members, that we were writing the book until five years down the road. We realized early on that completing the task of this book may never occur given the personal obstacles we encountered.

As with many manuscripts, we could not have done this without the support and encouragement of many people. We are incredibly grateful to the countless men and women who generously shared their combat and family experiences with us. We cried together, worried together, and hopefully, even healed a bit together.

We are equally grateful to those who gave their time to review the manuscript and provide us feedback and helpful suggestions. These included Faith Tardes, Dr. Leo Johnson, Dr. Patricia Wolfe, Becky Keigan, Dr. Janis DiCiacco, Dr. Gratia Meyer, Dr. Jerry Aschermann, Peggy Aschermann, John DiCiacco, and Dr. Rodney Haug of the Fort Collins Veteran's Administration. We are also deeply appreciative for the guidance and expertise of Karen Reddick, The Red Pen Editor and Karen Saunders and Kerrie Lian of MacGraphics Services for all their support in publishing a book that we hope will make a difference for veterans and their families.

Lastly, we could not have completed the manuscript without the constant encouragement of our immediate family members and close friends. Their hugs and positive presence helped us through some truly difficult moments. We are enormously grateful and humble to be blessed with our two sons, Chad and Christopher, who have grown into caring and vibrant young adults. Their special spirits made us a better family and far more compassionate individuals.

Silent Scream

You cannot see a Silent Scream
When looking from outside.
But you might find a glimpse of it
While peering deep in someone's eyes.

You will not hear a Silent Scream
In noisy, crowded rooms.
But if you sat down face to face
Your heart may sense its painful tune.

You shall not feel a Silent Scream
Amidst our fast-paced world.
But if you wandered near to it
Its anxious spirit might unfurl.

We walk right past a suffering soul
And often turn away.
Not strong enough to face the grief
This world has made him pay.

For Silent Screams are not unique
To those who fight and die.
The living warrior hell survived
Is left to hold his tears inside.

Janet J. Seahorn, Ph.D

Since the beginning of mankind,
warriors would leave their loved ones
and gallantly ride into battle.
Many returned victorious,
but often the scars of combat were deep.
The injury to the soul became known as
"Soldier's Heart, Shell Shock, Combat Fatigue, and PTSD".
War has its price.

-The Authors

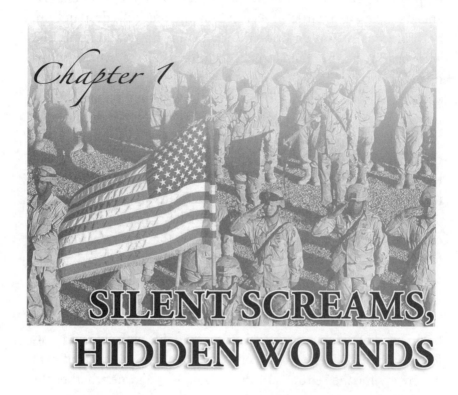

Chapter 1

SILENT SCREAMS, HIDDEN WOUNDS

If We Send Them, We Must Then Mend Them

"The world cannot be discovered by a journey of miles, no matter how long, but only a spiritual journey, a journey of one inch, very arduous and humbling and joyful, by which we arrive at the ground at our feet, and learn to be home."

—Wendell Berry

It is easy to ignore the full price a warrior pays for his participation in combat. Very few individuals, who have not experienced serving in a battle zone, can imagine the mass destruction, both physically and emotionally, it has on body and soul. The warrior's stories remain largely untold. Their sacrifices minimized or forgotten. Yet, the cost of war, whether fought centuries ago or today, is staggering. Never again will they regain the innocence that will be forever lost, nor can they forget the horrors of blood, death, and devastation. Therefore, if a country makes the choice to send its young men and women into battle, it must then be fully responsible to do everything in its power to mend the bodies, minds, spirits, and souls that return.

I have waited too long to begin this first chapter. Call it procrastination, fear, or possibly the uncertainty that our story mattered to anyone else. Perhaps my real problem was I didn't think anyone would want to read what I had to say. Hence, I am following my intuition and writing, if only for myself. Maybe putting thoughts down on paper will make me feel braver. I am not sure where to begin or what to focus on, because no part of life with a veteran suffering from PTSD is ever normal. Our story may have a different geography for the setting, but the trauma is the same whether the war is Vietnam, Iraq, or any past or present battlefield.

Photo on page 1 courtesy of U.S. Army

Tony with Vietnamese Orphan   Author's Collection

I am the wife of a man who served in combat as a young military officer and member of the Black Lions of the 1st Infantry Division. He had just turned twenty-one when deployed to Vietnam in early 1968, on the heels of the historic and devastating Tet Offensive. As a Second Lieutenant, he was assigned to the Big Red One as a Battalion Communications Officer. Following a brief combat engineering assignment, he took a command with the 2nd Battalion 28th Infantry Regiment, 1st Infantry Division. He was a member of the elite Black Lions, a battalion heavily decorated with battlefield honors dating back to World War I. The Black Lions were well known for their "esprit de corps" and willingness to lead combat missions into the heart of superior enemy forces. Their motto: "Duty First, No Mission Too Difficult, No Sacrifice Too Great" was not viewed lightly. Each member was trained in various elements of combat that allowed the unit to perform the most challenging of missions. With specialized training in several different fields related to combat, Tony was well prepared to serve with the Black Lions.

Within days of entering Vietnam, he shared a platform tent with two other men, both of whom had arrived in country on the same flight and had subsequently been assigned, along with Tony, to the 1st Infantry Division. On the third night, following their arrival in the Lai Khe base camp, a 122 mm Russian-made rocket exploded in the trees directly above their sleeping area. One of the fellow officers was killed by the shrapnel from the rocket exploding overhead while Tony was slightly wounded and the other young lieutenant sustained life threatening injuries. Tony's Vietnam experience in the midst of battles, on the ground and in the air continued for ten long months. He saw friends and comrades wounded and killed on numerous occasions, some dying in his arms as they took their last breath.

Toward the end of his tour he sustained shrapnel wounds to the chest and was shot twice in his right arm. He, along with a medic, placed a tourniquet on his upper arm to stop the bleeding. The intense battle raged on throughout the night; amazingly the tourniquet remained in place. Following dust-off (medivac out) the next day, Tony was flown to a field hospital. The doctors, seeing the massive contusion caused by the wound and prolonged tourniquet and fearing gangrene, insisted the arm must be amputated. Luckily, a few simple twists of fate saved his arm and began his road to recovery. In December 1968, he was air medivaced from Vietnam to a military hospital in Japan and then on to the United States for extended treatment and medical care. We met in the fall of 1969 and married in October of 1970. He seemed like a well-balanced, down-to-earth man. I had no idea of the depth and devastation of his experiences in Vietnam, and did not understand them for decades.

There was a quote I read from the government's mental health professionals about the adjustment problems counselors were noticing in returning Vietnam vets. Wow, "adjustment problems," what an understatement. Many of our veterans are facing more than adjustment problems. They are facing sleepless nights filled with the nightmares of flashback memories. They are confronted with the ghosts of dead, dying, and wounded men. Many are plagued with guilt, shame, grief, and despair. These feelings are not merely adjustment problems. They are problems entangled in emotional and physical survival.

One of the biggest insights I had while working on this book with Tony was how little I really understood about his combat experience. Oh, I was aware that he often had a short fuse, that he was overly anxious about small details, that he didn't sleep well, had vivid nightmares, and needed to always be in full control of many everyday schedules and activities. Sticking to his schedules seemed incredibly urgent to him. For example, when we went skiing on cold winter weekends, we would have to be up at the break of dawn and on the road quite early so we could avoid the traffic. Not a bad idea at the time, but trying to get two tired, young boys up, dressed, fed, and organized by 6:00 a.m. was no easy task.

Tony became anxious and visibly upset if the boys or I were not prepared to leave at the precise minute he had established the night before the outing. Tony took this delay as a personal dismissal of his authority. He shouted orders like an angry commanding officer, letting us know that we were making time on the road more dangerous and stressful. We had no clue why being on the road 10–15 minutes late was such a big deal. Weekend outings were supposed to be fun, a time to relax and enjoy each other as a family. Too many times these outings turned into shouting, crying, and upsetting occurrences.

Once on the road, Tony would calm down and for him everything was just fine. For the rest of us, however, we felt wounded, hurt, with stomachs tied in emotional knots, and a little less enthused about spending the day together. In our hearts we knew that Tony loved us deeply and would do anything for us, but in our minds we were not as sure.

If only during those times, we could have had an understanding of Post-Traumatic Stress Disorder, perhaps we would have made a stronger effort to be on time. Most of all, we would have understood that his behavior was not about us but about the demons he was fighting, and he did not, at the time, recognize these beasts or have the skills and strategies to act differently.

What we didn't know was that in Tony's mind, if we were late on the road, we would die. He learned this in Vietnam in so many crushingly severe, body-and-mind survival experiences. These experiences were later transferred to his life as a civilian once he was home. If we were late on the road we didn't think we would die, but Tony did. Not only did his mind believe this, but so did the unconscious feelings in his body. He had seen it happen many times. The memory was there whether he wanted it to be or not.

As a family, we definitely would have made healthier boundaries for ourselves, and been better able to protect ourselves against Tony's unpredictable behavior. Furthermore, he may have been able to see and/or feel the signs sooner, the emotional signals warning him that his outbursts were more a part of his past than a result of his present environment.

To this day, I am only familiar with a small part of his Vietnam nightmare. Though we had talked about his military service many times, I was dumbfounded by my lack of specific details and information. Recently, Tony was asked to do a presentation on his combat experience for a history class at our local university. During his preparation, he asked for some help with the slide show he wanted to include in the lecture. I thought I had seen most of his war photos, but several of these—the ones with the young men injured or dead, the ones with the helmets stuck on top of rifles with bayonet in the dirt to symbolize the death of fallen soldiers, the images with the incredible devastation of the terrain in the combat zones, the photos of downed helicopters, crumpled in pieces of tangled iron wedged between trees or burrowed deep into the earth from the horrific impact. These snapshots were new to me. They made me realize how little I did understand and how much I didn't know.

Perhaps this was because Tony didn't feel like sharing, or maybe it was easier for me not to ask, not to become too familiar with the tremendous trauma he suffered at such a young age. Perhaps he didn't trust himself, or me, enough to tell, and perhaps I didn't trust myself enough to touch the depth of his experience. Either way, it was all too obvious that a void existed between us for a very long time.

Military Service   Author's Collection

The empty space between reality and the safety of illusions that occupied our married life kept us somewhat emotionally protected. However, I am left to wonder what would have been different if we both had been able to go into those dark places sooner and face the demons directly.

In the early '70s we couldn't have done much more than we did because PTSD wasn't acknowledged or even identified as a legitimate medical diagnosis until the early '80s. We did as so many veterans and their families did for centuries—we lived as if nothing really happened. Once the veterans returned home, it was expected that everyone get on with life, no matter what.

Beauty Surrounding Trauma   Author's Collection

Don't ask. Don't tell. And most of all, don't remember! Life was to be lived as a pretend situation. Pretend that there wasn't a war. Pretend that once a warrior returned from combat, life was normal and stable. Pretend that young men and women didn't fight, die, and suffer wounds that were physical, psychological, and spiritual. Pretend as if the trauma was all a bad dream, a thing of the past, that time would eventually mend all wounds.

Only time didn't mend the wounds. Time only gave the wounds and the wounded extra years to feel different and psychologically traumatized without realizing why. Sometimes the wounds grew deeper and life lost its compass.

One might ask, why write a personal story about the long-term physical and psychological devastation of war? A story that isn't pleasurable to recall, and even more difficult to put into print. Elie Wiesel, a Jew who survived and wrote about the German concentration camps, put it this way:

Those who kept silent yesterday will remain silent tomorrow. The witness has forced himself to testify. For the youth of tomorrow, for the children who will be born tomorrow. He does not want his past to become their future.

—Elie Wiesel, *Night*, 1972, xiii

Books with challenging personal stories are not so much about the messenger, but more importantly, the significance of the message itself. The message that human suffering cannot, and should not, ever go unnoticed or be forgotten is crucial for present and future generations because forgetfulness will chip away at a culture, a nation, an individual's humanity, slowly eroding the fabric of what makes men, as well as nations: Caring sentries of the soul and spirit.

Coping With Many Personalities

PTSD is like living with Dr. Jekyll and Mr. Hyde. One moment things are fine, and the next all hell is breaking loose. As a spouse, I didn't always recognize the triggers when Tony "lost it," that it wasn't my fault. My actions had very little to do with his *reactions*. I did not know how to help erase the suffering he endured. To compensate, I converted into less of me to the point of becoming seriously ill.

Our sons had even less understanding of their Dad's behaviors. Like me, they thought that it must, in some way, be their fault. They were merely children, not miniature soldiers. They could never be orderly enough, quiet enough, compliant enough to subdue Dad's demons. What they sometimes felt, however, was that they were not good enough to keep Dad from being upset and angry. They could not be the competent, compliant military troops who marched to the beat of an unseen foe. This was a difficult burden for a young child.

According to Tori Deangelis in her article, "Helping Families Cope with PTSD", the burden on families living with a combat vet experiencing Post-Traumatic Stress tends to "wreck havoc on intimate relationships" (*Monitor on Psychology,* January 2008, 44). Domestic violence is three times more common in veterans with PTSD. A report by psychologist Dr. Candice Monson, deputy director of the women's health science division of the National Center for Post-Traumatic Stress Disorder states, "evidence fingers PTSD as one of the mental health conditions most likely to lead to relationship problems because sufferers become reclusive, not wanting to attend various family/social events, and conflicts are fueled by excess anger and irritability in the vet." In addition, Dr. Monson adds that "the vet may tend to be 'over controlling' and demanding of their children's behaviors due to unrealistic fears about the children's safety" (*Monitor on Psychology,* January 2008, 44).

Wounded warriors, therefore, must acknowledge that their painful experiences do not end with them. Left unacknowledged, the damage these traumas wreak on those around them will continue. What is crucial for the warrior to understand is this:

It is not your fault you had to endure such anguish. It is not your fault that your mind, body, and soul now carry the wounds. It is not your fault that you continue to experience flashbacks, panic attacks, and sensations of dread. It is, however, your responsibility to confront the effects of the trauma, for if you don't, we as spouses, offspring, and friends cannot help you. We cannot know what you refuse to reveal. We cannot support what we do not understand. Only you, the wounded warrior, can and must take the first steps— the first steps toward healing—the first steps toward a better life. The first steps toward keeping those who love you most safe from your unpredictable and unexplainable outbursts of impatience and rage.

The intention of this book is to support you and other wounded warriors as you face the trauma from combat and recover your compass. You may ask the questions: Can I grieve my experience as it affected me then and as it affects me now? Will it ever get better? The answer: Absolutely! If you can muster the courage and insight to get help, then you can weep, grieve, and mend.

If this healing mission could be done alone, it would have been done centuries ago. Trauma would not be a part of our modern world. Yet, it still exists, and at a considerable level. Not everyone succumbs to the demons. Some wounded heal, even if the scars remained. You can too. It is a journey that will not be easy or swift. But it is a journey that can be managed with support, knowledge, perseverance, and prayer.

Focus, Persist, Conquer, Live!

Author's Collection

"Remember, some miracles take time. Adversity does not lead us away from our best ambitions, but closer to them.

The impossible just takes a little longer"

—Art Berg

Serenity Prayer

Lord grant me the serenity to accept the things I cannot change,
The courage to change the things I can,
And the wisdom to know the difference.

Hope   Author's Collection

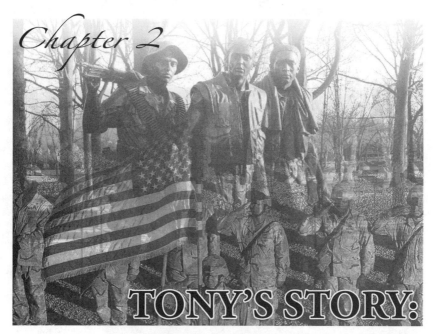

Chapter 2

TONY'S STORY: VIETNAM 1968

We were the *Dauntless Black Lions*

*Warrior descendants from the battle grounds of Cantigny.
Named for our fierce combat, beginning and continuing
since our triumphant victories during World War I. The
legacy continued throughout World War II and Korea.*

*Now, more than halfway through the twentieth century,
beyond the mid 1960s, we carried that reputation into the
remote jungles of a land faraway.*

Vietnam.

**"Duty First, No Mission Too Difficult,
No Sacrifice Too Great"**

-1st Infantry Division
(Big Red One)

Author's Collection

1st Infantry Division   *Black Lions*

The Journey

We were young and full of hope, practically invincible. . .or so we believed.

I will never forget how innocent she looked in her patriotic red, white, and blue flight attendant uniform. Her long auburn hair flowed over her petite shoulders as she moved down the aisle, perky and full of life. She too was young, about my own age and could easily have been a college cheerleader. We talked casually in the aisle as she performed her repetitious and seemingly nonstop duties in the professional manner for which she was trained—pushing carts of food and beverages, handing out reading materials, ensuring all aboard were comfortable and reasonably content. And, of course, as we nonchalantly made eye contact, I waited wishfully for her to whisper softly in my ear, "coffee, tea or me." But, only in my wildest dreams!

Beyond her striking attractiveness, I became equally intrigued with how kind and caring she truly was. Certainly easier to know than the same person you might accidentally meet on the street back home, yet somewhat guarded in how she responded. For a full day and night we talked as she worked while the journey continued with the low drone of the engines bringing us ever closer to our destiny.

For what seemed a blissful eternity, passing through the International Date Line, moving constantly westward toward a land I had never seen. The flight went on and on. We were young, gung-ho military officers flying twenty-two hours from Los Angeles to the tropics of Southeast Asia. Not knowing and unknowing what would eventually lie ahead. After brief refueling stops in Hawaii and the Philippines, we approached our destination. The airline captain broke the monotonous silence with his calm commanding announcement.

"We are descending altitude into Ben Hoa Province in the Republic of South Vietnam. The current surface ground temperature is a balmy 108 degrees, with 98 percent humidity." I looked at the guy next to me in what must have appeared as initial shock. "One hundred and eight degrees!"

The captain's voice changed slightly. His next words were spoken very slowly, with a boost of confidence.

"Godspeed to each and every one of you. I look forward to seeing you in twelve months on your return flight home."

It wasn't long before the plane touched down and we taxied across the tarmac. The scene outside the plane's tiny window flashed by slowly, with a seemingly endless mass of military vehicles, supplies, and men. Olive drab was the obvious uniform of the day. Everything, man and machine, were clad in military green: all on a mission, scurrying around in jungle fatigues, looking as if a war was going on.

My fantasy airline attendant began crying as we came to a stop and the plane door eventually opened to allow our final disembarking. At first, I didn't understand. Was she sad to see us go?

As I moved forward and took my first step down the off-loading ramp, the reality of Vietnam hit me squarely in the face. The temperature and humidity took my breath away. The thick, hot air made my heart pound as an eerie sensation came over me.

I squinted into the bright sunlight, still choking on the humidity as I tried to catch my breath.

And then I saw them. The rectangular boxes lined up in military formation for the return trip home. We, the live warriors, were about to be replaced on the plane with the dead warriors. They were, without knowing, statistics of those who had served their country and made, without judgment, the ultimate sacrifice.

Silent Warriors   VA002917, Bryan Grigsby Collection, Vietnam Archive, TTU

Heat waves rippled above their cold, lifeless, boxed forms like a mirage. Transport from the military morgue to the awaiting cargo hold of the plane was but a short distance away. Maybe what I was seeing wasn't real, maybe this was simply a bad dream.

I looked back. The flight attendant's tears of anguish rolled down her ashen cheeks.

She had been here before.

This introduction to my Vietnam tour of duty is a tribute to the thousands of troops who served in combat, fought and died alongside friends and comrades. It is also an acknowledgment of those who lived and survived to return home and the reality they faced long after the cries of battle had ended. For many of us who were "lucky" enough to survive the battlefields, we eventually learned that often our wounds are permanent. The scars of combat, both physically and mentally, may never heal. The journey home may likely be a journey that lasts a lifetime.

The story that follows is not fiction, nor is it a story about winning or losing, but rather a story about warriors returning from battle, how they live their lives after combat and their subsequent influence and impact on families and friends. This is my story, which is written simply from my perspective, based on my experience, and does not necessarily represent all veterans returning from war.

Of the many with whom I served, some of their given birth names or military code names I remember. Most I cannot recall, or have long forgotten.

For some who serve in combat, and specifically based on my experience from serving in Vietnam, there was no celebrated homecoming, no parade to honor those who served so valiantly. Most returned instead to a kind of embarrassed silence, as if they had done something shameful, and no one wanted to talk about it.

Many have paid a terrible patriotic price for serving their country. Stunted careers, shattered marriages, physical and mental scars that refuse to heal have been far more common than anyone could have possibly known or anticipated.

When I first started putting my thoughts down on paper, I began with the misconception that this was just about my experience as a young military officer serving his country, doing the right thing. It did not take long for me to realize that most of my reflection on Vietnam, and my experiences while serving in combat, were not simply about me at all. They were about loss— as a young man, as a family, and more broadly, as a society. My perspective is written ultimately and specifically about the impact war has on those who serve in combat and survive. That is the only story I know. My journey home continues.

Soldiers returning from battle will never view living, suffering, and death the same again. Loved ones who suffer alongside veterans who have lived through the combat experience are, in many cases, traumatized as well. None will ever view life's trials and challenges the same way. Men killing men. Or more accurately, human beings killing human beings. War rarely distinguishes men from boys, women from children. Do not confuse patriotism with the realities of war. There are very few individuals more patriotic than veterans.

Those who would only find glory in war have spent little time in a combat zone. Who is the enemy? What is the enemy? In many instances, friend one day and foe the next. Here we are today in the twenty-first century, still killing one another for our own just cause. Each believing our mission is justified. Our cause is noble.

How barbaric.

The Reality of War   VA004349, Douglas Pike Collection, Vietnam Archive, TTU

As young soldiers we lived the dreams of most American youth, full of hope, full of ambitions; growing up in the land of plenty. High school football pep rallies, bonfires, and sports victories were all a part of who we were. We were practically invincible in our own right. Little did we know how quickly that dream would fade into the reality of war.

Now, as I reflect back, the nightmares probably began in my subconscious the moment we stepped off the plane onto the tarmac at Tan Son Nhut airport in Bien Hoa, north of Saigon. A place called Vietnam was a common newspaper headline, yet remained a far away place we could not accurately or clearly define. Somehow here we were, as if transported through a time machine from yesterday to today, in less than a heartbeat. Almost overnight we had been transformed from All-American athletes to combat warriors of destiny.

South Vietnam

South Vietnam   Author's Collection

The naiveté of American youth comes from not knowing or anticipating life's unforgiving traumas. During the 1960s, when I was growing up, sports and girls were my major priorities. Sure, I heard and read about a place called Vietnam and knew that America was involved at some liaison level in keeping communism from spreading, but beyond that, I knew very little about the history or plight of the Vietnamese people or America's political and military involvement. Even today, most Americans who have not served in combat or are otherwise associated with combat, are naïve and relatively ambivalent about the tragedies of war. They are, simply, too far removed and isolated from the atrocities that exist elsewhere and more commonly throughout the world.

Deplaning at Tan Son Nhut, we, the new guys or New Bs (new blood), even as young military officers trained as leaders of men, were shocked into the reality of war when we saw the flight cargo bins being loaded with the Grim Reaper's endless caravan of body bags. That was not how we had envisioned our return trip back to "The World." When I think about that initial shocking experience, I often believe it was only a hallucination played out in the darkest corners of my mind. It is only when I awake at night in a cold sweat, heart pounding, that I realize the dreams are, in fact, reality.

Military Career

My army career started in the fall of 1966. I was in college at the University of Wyoming. Finances were running low and like many college students, I remained unclear about my higher education interests and ultimate career objectives. After changing majors for the third time, I decided a new direction was needed. Following a chance visit to the campus Air Force recruiter, we carved out a strategic plan that would not only give me some much needed direction, but would also answer my college and career objectives. I would become a member of the military elite. I would become an Air Force fighter pilot!

The recruiter drafted a contract between me and the United States Air Force. There was only one slight condition, which at the time seemed irrelevant. There was a two month waiting list to get into the special program. The government, per our mutual agreement, would pay for my remaining college. I would enroll in Air Force ROTC. Following graduation, as a newly commissioned Second Lieutenant, I would be off to my prescribed flight training program. The letter of agreement called for a six year active military commitment following college. This certainly wasn't an issue for me since I'd surely make a career out of flying. I had often dreamed as a youngster that one day I might become a pilot. I just had never believed the dream would become a reality. Now at last it all made perfect sense. My dad, all of my uncles, and many other family members were military veterans from World War II and Korea. I would serve in their footsteps. Even beyond that, I would fly!

I decided to take a few months off to work, earn some much needed cash, and wait for my Air Force induction date. In less than thirty days, I received a draft notice to report to Uncle Sam's ARMY enlistment office in Denver, Colorado.

My world came crashing down. How could this possibly happen? Didn't the Army understand? I was already committed to serve my country. I had already signed the paperwork.

It didn't matter. Uncle Sam had already decided I was Army material. In other words, I added to the draft induction quota.

Author's Collection

Acceptance to Officer Candidate School

Following basic training at Fort Bliss, Texas and advanced individual training (AIT) at Fort Leonard Wood, Missouri, I soon learned that I had qualified for Officer Candidate School (OCS) at Fort Gordon, Georgia. After months, which seemed more like an eternity of intense military strategy and indoctrination training, I graduated as a newly commissioned officer. Of the one hundred or so candidates who began the school, less than thirty graduated. Being one of the few who somehow survived the rigorous program, I now carried the new rank of Second Lieutenant.

Following OCS, I applied for the career officer program and flight school, all in an attempt to further my aspirations as a career officer and eventual military pilot. Six months later, upon rapid completion of intensified training and certification, I received orders for Vietnam.

After a short leave of absence to visit family in Wyoming, and followed by a brief but memorable night on the town in San Diego with one of my best

Officer Candidate School Graduate-Tony   Author's Collection

friends, the local police decided that I would be given the choice of sleeping off the remainder of the night in the local pokey or boarding a flight to the Far East. With that ultimatum, I used my better military judgment and reported to the deployment center in Los Angeles, California.

The next day I boarded a charter flight with fellow officers for a twenty-two-hour trip to the tropics of Southeast Asia. My military orders were general in nature, and simply stated I would receive further instructions for deployment to a military unit upon arrival in Vietnam. Young army officers appeared to be in demand, yet highly expendable element of the war. And demand often exceeded supply. I was hopeful of receiving assignment to an aircraft or air-mobile unit to further my career ambitions as a pilot. At the same time, I also realized my previous military training included expertise in demolitions, combat engineering, and field communications. In a war

VA037747, Lee Baker Collection, Vietnam Archive, TTU

Military Memorial

of attrition it became increasingly apparent that many fields of expertise were in demand, some more than others.

After trying, but failing to negotiate what I considered to be my best options for unit assignment, I was matter-of-factly informed that my Vietnam military placement would be with the 1st Infantry Division, headquartered in Lai Khe, about ninety klicks (kilometers) north of Saigon. The 1st Infantry Division (Big Red One), better known by the troops as the Bloody Red One, had taken a terrible beating early in the New Year as a mass of Viet Cong and NVA troops had hit the unit with an endless bombardment of 122 mm rockets, mortar, and small arms fire. The Tet Offensive had taken its toll. As a result, a majority of the new personnel that came into country were sent to replace casualties.

Convoy   VAS008066, William Autrey Collection, Vietnam Archive, TTU

I loaded my AWOL (absent without leave) bag into a deuce and a half (2 ½ ton cargo truck) and headed north in a military escorted convoy. The three-hour drive would follow a portion of the infamous Highway 13, more accurately called Thunder Road. As the red dust and sweat coated our bodies and created an appearance of battle weary forces, our vehicle parade slowly moved away from the hustle/bustle of Ben Hoa and metropolitan Saigon.

Moving North   VAS004626, Larry Stone Collection, Vietnam Archive, TTU

Our outward disguise was little comfort for the inexperience and uncertainty we felt inside. Although much of the foliage along the road had been cleared by the rolling thunder-like sound of B-52 strikes, thus the road's name, we still remained vigilant for the common roadside ambushes and booby traps. For most of us, it wasn't until years later that we began to hear and see the effects of a defoliating chemical also used to clear Thunder Road—Agent Orange.

Thunder Road   Author's Collection

Agent Orange   VA002930, Bryan Grigsby Collection, Vietnam Archive, TTU

Finally, in a cloud of dust, the convoy arrived at its destination, Division Headquarters. Lai Khe, 1st Infantry Division base of operations and home for the next year.

Nightmares of Battle

The 1st Infantry Division had chosen Lai Khe because it was strategically located in an abandoned French rubber plantation on a direct line between Cambodia and Saigon, the South Vietnam capital. Lai Khe was on the Ho Chi Min Trail, a major enemy supply and troop infiltration route into the South. Although a few villas and other buildings were scattered throughout the compound, most of the Division's living quarters consisted of tents on platforms and sandbag bunkers. Not what I considered a good sign.

Lai Khe   Author's Collection

I was initially assigned to Headquarters Company, essentially a staging assignment, prior to further deployment into the field with a combat unit. While performing various duties with HQC and awaiting assignment, I took on the construction of a new underground operations center. The Headquarters Operations Center that existed when I arrived consisted of a wood frame building with lots of shrapnel holes. Incoming 122 mm rockets and mortar fire were common occurrences, often daily at Lai Khe.

Like most New Bs, I had little idea what to expect as we prepared for search and destroy missions along the Cambodian border infiltration routes. I learned as much as possible from battle tested and hardened troops, and made friends with several individuals with previous combat experience. I saw that short timers, those who only had about a month left in Vietnam, did not sleep in open, unfortified tents. They preferred bunkers with high sandbag walls and a fortified roof. On day three of my tour in Lai Khe, I learned why.

Around midnight, as we slept, an incoming 122 mm rocket hit the rubber tree canopy above my canvas tent platform and exploded. Having a 122 mm Russian-made missile explode overhead, as I soon learned, was the worse possible scenario for a rocket blast. The red hot piercing shrapnel mushroomed and penetrated everything in its destructive path below. Only fate determined who survived or who died.

I was one of the lucky ones. A single fragment of shrapnel pierced my leg. Others were not as lucky. I will never forget the screams of horror in the night from my bunkmates. One lost an arm and both legs. The third one died. Welcome to Vietnam.

"We lie under the network of arching shells and live in a suspense of uncertainty. If a shot comes, we can duck, that is all; we neither know nor can determine where it will fall."

—Erich Maria Remarque, *All Quiet On The Western Front*

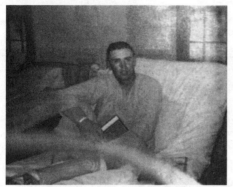

Author's Collection
Hospital in Long Bien-Tony

VA035492, Garnett Bell Collection, Vietnam Archive, TTU
Coming Home

This initiation into war did not drive me apart from the others; it brought me closer. Early in my tour of duty, I had been bloodied. While I had unquestionably been more fortunate than others, the horrific shock that rang out in the night did not end. To this day the ringing in my ears reminds me constantly of that dark night, suddenly disrupted so very early in my Vietnam experience. Maybe the entire experience was just a horrible nightmare? But, many more nightmares would follow.

For the first couple of months, while assigned to headquarters, I seized every possible opportunity to get into the field. Not only to escape the "sitting duck" attitude pervasive within the headquarters compound, but more specifically to satisfy the desire to charge headlong into the true combat experience for which I had so diligently trained. As a result, I elected to participate in various reconnaissance and resupply flights to outlying patrols operating throughout our sector of responsibility. Depending upon the level of enemy contact, our air mobile support would respond accordingly. Some days we flew a sortie with other choppers, on other days we flew alone. Given the option, when flying solo, we would always elect to fly a UH-1B gunship for the extra security of additional fire power.

Sortie   VA050700, Americal Division Veterans Association Collection,
                                             Vietnam Archive, TTU

Solo Flight   VAS049375, Charles E. Rogers Collection, Vietnam Archive, TTU

The most prominent point in our area of operation, the Iron Triangle, was a towering, ominous looking mountain called Nui Ba Dien. Though U.S. forces occupied a command post atop the battle-scarred and ghostly mountain, Charlie (the Viet Cong) was said to control the rest. Throughout were tunnels, bunkers, ammunition dumps, and the ever-present booby traps. On a clear night the dark peak, known locally by U.S. troops as the Black Virgin Mountain, came alive with a network of lights reminiscent of fireflies on a timbered hillside. The VC were busy in their unending pursuit of reestablishing communications and re-supplying forces.

Nui Ba Dien Above Cloud Cover   VAS042495, Richard D. Besley Collection, Vietnam Archive, TTU

I flew several times to the mystery mountain, mostly with supplies, but on one specific occasion, I went to replace battle-weary troops with new recruits. Those who had the dubious responsibility of manning the mountaintop often appeared to be in a state of hardened disbelief at the fact they were finally leaving. Always listening for the pop, pop of mortar tubes and constant barrage of enemy artillery, sniper, and mortar fire will do that to a person. Always listening through the constant rustling of the prevailing winds: listening, anticipating, waiting, dying.

Battle Weary   Author's Collection

Sometime in late June, I received a letter from home. Mail from home was always a temporary escape from the demands of war. On this occasion the news was anything but uplifting. Two of my best friends from high school and college had been killed in a head-on car crash while returning to National Guard summer camp. They had not volunteered to go to Vietnam, but, in their own way, were still providing a service to their country. Now they were gone. Life, unquestionably, throws some curves, and is unpredictable at best.

Unfortunately, I had little time to mourn or reflect before returning to my own reality.

Shortly thereafter, on another seemingly routine flight near the eastern section of III Corp, we received communication that a recon patrol near Quan Loi had walked into an enemy horseshoe ambush and was in dire need of air support. On this particular day we were flying a Huey slick with only M–60 door gunners for fire power. I established communications with the command center, which put me in direct contact with the recon platoon leader. With wounded on the ground, the unit was withdrawing to a clearing where we could land and dust-off the casualties. In less than a minute from popping smoke we set down and loaded three of the most seriously wounded.

As we began our liftoff, AK-47 fire hit us from the tree line. Almost instantaneously, we took a direct hit from an RPG (rocket propelled grenade). The chopper went down in a plume of smoke. Somehow the impact catapulted me from the downed chopper. Somersaulting helplessly through the smoke-filled air, I landed in a daze on my neck and back. As I opened my eyes in disbelief I saw that I was drenched in oil and jet fuel, lying about

Down Chopper   VA000202, Douglas Pike Collection, Vietnam Archive, TTU

twenty feet from the chopper. I remember looking down at my outstretched hands. They were sticky and covered with something red. Blood.

Before I regained my senses, the downed chopper exploded in flames. I scrambled away, alone. For reasons still unknown to me, of those onboard, I was the only one to survive. The blood on my hands scarred my soul.

The blood was real, but it was not mine.

Shortly thereafter, a helicopter squadron responding as well to the imperiled patrol's call for help appeared on the scene. With Huey Cobras laying down heavy perimeter firepower, several choppers were able to set down in a nearby clearing and extract the remaining troops, including me.

VA011585, Dominick Cirincione
Collection, Vietnam Archive, TTU

Huey Iroquois Medivac and
Huey Cobra Gunship

Troop Extraction   VA040233, Glenn Helm Collection, Vietnam Archive, TTU

The Nightmare Continues

By mid-spring new military operations were added to the bloody drawing board, which ultimately led to my field assignment with the 2nd Battalion 28th Infantry, 1st Infantry Division—Black Lions.

We were the proud members of the Big Red One, the 1st Infantry Division and the elite Black Lions of the 2nd Battalion of the 28th Infantry Regiment. The battalion was heavy with battle-field honors dating back to World War I. Our motto: Duty First, No Mission Too Difficult, No Sacrifice Too Great.

Only a few short months earlier, during October 1967, a battalion of the 2nd of the 28th Black Lions had encountered a superior force of 1,400 Viet Cong. Of the 142 Black Lions participating in the search-and-destroy mission, 58 died. Nearly every remaining member of the elite unit was wounded. What became known as the battle of Ong Thanh, also served as one of the most bloody and deadly operations for the Black Lions and of the Vietnam War. Facing the challenges of combat, with a total commitment of call-to-duty, was not a concept unfamiliar to the Black Lions, both past and present.

The Big Red One's area of operation covered War Zone C and a portion of D, stretching north from Saigon to the Cambodian border and a corridor to the east and west that encompassed major enemy infiltration routes into South Vietnam and ultimately Saigon. The Black Lions were primarily assigned to the northern sector from Lai Khe to the border. Our mission was to encounter the enemy, estimate their strength, and report the data back to headquarters. The objective was clearly to disrupt enemy movement, maximize body count, and direct firepower to allow B-52s, F-4 fighters, and artillery to do their designed work of devastation.

B-52

B-52 Air Strike   Author's Collection

F-4s

Air Strike on Perimeter of Fire Support Base   Author's Collection

The Vietnamese New Year in January 1968, more commonly referenced as Tet, was the benchmark for the Big Red One's military strategies in the general vicinity of what became known as the Iron Triangle. The historic Tet Offensive would become the basis for which future operations would concentrate, what was commonly referred to as the "Lessons of Tet." With little time to waste, my service with the Black Lions brought me closer to the soldiers than anything you can imagine. Our mission success and ultimately our own survival would depend on thoroughly deployed troops who were dedicated, well trained and committed to the orders of the day. Anything less would spell disaster. Disaster in this case was simple: death.

All of us placed an unspoken trust in one another; our lives depended on it. After all, what other possession was more precious? We were truly a band of brothers bonded by a common cause. The threat of constant death made us even more alive. We were warriors!

The Big Red One was spread across the country and participated in many different supporting missions. Our division worked with various other units, all focused on locating the enemy and disrupting their insurgent strategies. During the spring and summer of 1968, following the Tet Offensive, most of the Big Red One's operations involved search and destroy missions. We would fly into known or suspected enemy occupied areas and attempt to make contact. Many of these operations could be characterized as a war of attrition—make contact and maximize body count.

Boarding a C-130-Tony   Author's Collection

Most missions were of platoon or company-sized encounters. Many such patrols resulted in ambush with resulting body count, friend or foe, used as the determinant of which side won or lost.

Troop Movement   Author's Collection

By October, however, the strategy of our missions and the nature of the war began to make a monumental change. Intelligence reports indicated that mass forces of NVA (North Vietnamese Army) soldiers were moving southward through Cambodia toward South Vietnam and the Black Lions' corridor of responsibility. As a member of Headquarters Staff Operations for the Black Lions, we began to plan Operation Fishhook, one of the bloodiest battles of the war.

Huey Slick - Tony   Author's Collection

The mission was to fly within a few klicks (kilometers) of the Cambodian border and carve a NDP (Night Defensive Position) out of unexplored jungle. My role as Battalion Communications Officer was to fly the first sortie into the remote area, offload troops on the ground, and provide air-ground-air communication for the remainder of the battalion-light insertion. NDP Julie, as it became known and later referred to as FSB Julie (Fire Support Base) was established on a major and immediate North Vietnamese Army infiltration route into the heart of South Vietnam. The Black Lions, a battalion-light of 160 men, established operations in the midst of an estimated four regiments of 3,000 NVA regulars. We were to become decoys for the infiltrating enemy forces.

We were the bait, like goats tethered to attract lions. I think back on how ironic it was that we were called the Black Lions.

Air Mobile   VAS039779, William Bruce Bartow Collection, Vietnam Archive, TTU

Hot Landing Zone (LZ)   Author's Collection

CH-47 Supply Drop   Author's Collection

Operations Planning - Tony and Battalion Staff   Author's Collection

FSB Julie   Author's Collection

The plan was to make contact with the enemy once they moved across the border and then allow our air and artillery power to take over. The plan worked only too well, or as war strategists would later claim, "Better than expected."

Daily, for the first week, we were plagued with rocket, mortar, and sniper fire. We also ran ambush patrols outside our position to determine enemy activity. Halfway through that first week, we "secretly" flew a LRRP (Long Range Reconnaissance Patrol) team across the border into Cambodia in an effort to better access enemy strength. Almost immediately the LRRPs made enemy contact and radioed for pickup. They were under intense fire, and the dense triple-canopy jungle did not render many clearings for chopper landings. I was manning the battalion radios from my remote command center when it became obvious the LRRPs had no possibility of making it back to Julie alive if they withdrew on foot.

Troop Insertion   VA002367, Douglas Pike Collection, Vietnam Archive, TTU

Jungle Patrol   VA035917, Willliam Foulke Collection, Vietnam Archive, TTU

Search & Destroy Mission   VA002494, Bryan Grigsby Collection, Vietnam
Archive, TTU

One of my fellow officers on combat-ready standby jumped into one of the Hueys based at our small jungle outpost. Within minutes he had spotted the retreating LRRPs with a mass of NVA in hot pursuit. At least four of the retreating members were able to board the chopper before it took on ground fire. The chopper, momentarily, climbed to safety. Then, within seconds, it was engulfed in smoke and just as quickly plummeted back to earth. All I could see above the jungle tree line was a ball of fire and smoke. The chopper filled the northern sky with black smoke until dark.

Two days later, one of our recon patrols reached the crash site, less than a half klick from our position. They saw the chopper's charred skeleton with the bodies of the dead hanging from its ghastly remains. After a hasty search of the immediate area, the patrol was driven back by small arms fire and returned to the relative safety of Julie's encampment. Due to the overwhelming numbers of enemy troops in the area, no further attempt was made to recover bodies or search for survivors. Surely some of the LRRP patrol was reported as MIA or possible POWs. Could we have done more? The memory is still one of many nightmares that haunt me.

On October 25, almost a week after Julie was carved out of the dense jungle, the NVA main force decided to attack our position in an all-out suicide assault. The intensity of the initial bombardment made direct hits on several of our positions, which resulted in multiple American casualties. Five young soldiers in a small entrenchment, not ten yards from my command post, took a direct hit from the first barrage; all died instantly.

In the distance, mortar tubes popped and NVA trucks rumbled along the Ho Chi Min Trail. Thousands of NVA were coming our way, headed directly for our defensive position. Behind the endless incoming of enemy fire, flares began to outline the images of NVA troops as they approached our perimeter, and continued their massive assault into our small, undermanned outpost. Like ghosts, the enemy continued their endless assault, emerging from the smoky dark of night only temporarily illuminated by Spooky aircraft flares.

Artillery support from FSB Rita, located 15 klicks to the south, was established to support our operation and became our only salvation. Some artillery rounds landed just beyond our perimeter as planned, while other rounds fell short of their intended target and exploded within our concertina wire; more commonly referred to as "friendly fire."

Intense combat lasted throughout the night and ended at daylight when Army Cobras and Air Force fighters were able to intercede and help fortify our position. In addition to the numerous Black Lions who were killed or wounded, the enemy dead were stacked like cordwood around our perimeter and throughout Julie. Several of those killed inside our position had died from hand-to-hand combat.

In the days that followed, a constant bombardment of B-52 air strikes, F-4 fighters, and Huey gun ships strafed the area around us. Attempts to dust-off the wounded or re-supply Julie, resulted in mortar and small arms fire. Several dust-off choppers took direct hits from small arms and RPG fire and were ground-

Devastation at FSB Julie
Author's Collection

Captured Enemy Arms Author's Collection

ed within our perimeter. There was enough death and destruction at FSB Julie to satisfy any war or warrior for a lifetime.

Operation Fishhook became a turning point for the Black Lions. Many of the old soldiers, both enlisted and officers, had served their tour of duty and were leaving. Many others were casualties of the battle, either dead or wounded, and had to be replaced. Fresh new recruits were arriving daily and tasting their first blood of battle. And still others arrived under the stench of the recent carnage and were learning firsthand the reality of war. Following duty at Julie, our bloody work finished, many returned to base camp at Lai Khe for a much needed rest. Unfortunately, due to a shortage of officers, I relocated, along with my staff operations personnel, a short distance south to FSB Rita where the carnage continued. The NVA were relentless in their southerly movement toward Saigon.

Combat Zone   VA034766, Ronald Garrison Collection, Vietnam Archive, TTU

Killed in Action (KIA)   VA040236, Glenn Helm Collection, Vietnam Archive, TTU

After Julie and Rita, following daily artillery and B-52 air strikes, much of the opposing NVA Division had dispersed and the Black Lions began to move from one sector of III Corp to another, establishing new Fire Support Bases, and duplicating the tactics and strategy that had proven so successful at Julie.

R&R (Rest & Recuperation) was always a welcome break from the rigors of combat. Unfortunately, every time I was scheduled to go on R&R my duties required my participation in the next mission of the Black Lions. I did, however, find one opportunity to escape to Saigon for two days and spend time with a friend from high school who was stationed with the air force. The only "condition" required of my commanding officer was to fill the chopper with captured AK-47 rifles and trade them for new PRC-25 field radios. Most of our ra-

FSB Rita   Author's Collection

dios were shot, literally, and needed to be replaced. Bartering is often a necessity in a combat zone!

Captured AK-47-Tony   Author's Collection

Flying to Saigon to Trade
AK-47s for Combat Field
Radios

Author's Collection

51

Tony and High School Friend in Saigon   Author's Collection

Bronze of ARVN-Tony   Author's Collection

In the area known as the Trapezoid, we made countless air assaults, and each operation resulted in making contact with the enemy. During November, we established a new FSB in an expanse of elephant grass that later became known as Cantigny II.

The grass was so tall it was impossible to determine where the foliage ended and the solid earth began. I took the first flight into the LZ, with the objective of establishing the initial communication center on the ground in the center of an open clearing. As we approached the pre-identified landing zone, our chopper immediately sustained intense NVA small arms fire. While attempting to set down in the hot LZ, my radio man took a small arms round through the mouth. Hovering above the tall grass, we were sitting ducks. We had few choices, remain on board and be killed, or jump and hope for survival on the ground. We jumped!

Jumping From Chopper   VA036946, Charles Anderson Collection,
                                          Vietnam Archive, TTU

The chopper was fifteen feet above the top of the elephant grass, and the grass was almost fifteen feet tall. After falling for what seemed an eternity, approximately the height of a two-story building, we hit the ground and were immediately surrounded by enemy troops. They were talking and shouting all around us, yet were unable to pinpoint our exact location in the towering grass.

Taking Cover in Elephant Grass   VA000943 Douglas Pike Collection,
Vietnam Archive, TTU

Huey Cobra   VAS039777, William Bruce Bartow Collection,
Vietnam Archive, TTU

Off in the distance, I heard the distinct wop, wop of a Huey Cobra gunship. I immediately popped smoke to disclose our position to the chopper. Almost instantaneously, we were completely surrounded by a massive burst of mini guns, followed by a devastating barrage of explosives from rocket pods. The Cobra firepower was precise and deadly. With little room for error, the pilot had come through with flawless precision. Although injured and wounded, we had somehow made it through an almost impossible situation.

Soon F-4 fighters entered the battle and the hot LZ was finally prepped and cleared for further troop landings. The area was eventually secured and another FSB would be carved out of the jungle. We would live to fight another day.

The Final Battle

Following our operation at Cantigny, where we continued to get pounded, losing more troops to the casualty of war, we moved to another tactical area that would be my last assignment in South Vietnam. A year earlier, the Big Red One had fought and secured the same piece of real estate—temporarily. Once again the unit was back fighting to regain familiar territory. Same place, different soldiers. After only three days of operations out of FSB Junction City, we were bombarded one more time with an overwhelming night assault from a superior NVA force.

Fire Support Base Supplies   Author's Collection

Artillery Support   Photo Courtesy of U. S. Army, Staff Sgt. Joselito Aribuabo

Air Mobile Troop Extraction   VA000751, Douglas Pike Collection,
Vietnam Archive, TTU

Around midnight, with virtually no warning, I was wounded in the chest and right arm from the initial barrage, and continued to maintain position and coordinate air and artillery fire support while the battle raged throughout the night. The night sky was eerie with a dense fog as air support was initially grounded and then somehow managed to locate our position and suppress the enemy assault. Next morning, following dust-off of several flights of dead and critically wounded, I was medivaced to Long Bien, and then, once medically stabilized, sent to a U.S. military hospital near Yokohama, Japan. My tour of duty in Vietnam was over!

Back Home

A few months later while recovering at Fitzsimmons Army Hospital in Denver, Colorado, I had my first panic attack. I thought I was having a terrible nightmare only to realize the feeling of despair was real and not imagined. At first I thought I was experiencing a reaction to the many injections of morphine and other pain killers, but the feeling of hopelessness would not subside. Apparently, as a coping mechanism while in combat, I had subconsciously created a mental barrier that allowed me to isolate my emotions from the realities of war. During combat, we had to put aside our emotions in order to survive. We had to focus on what was immediately happening, not on what had happened previously.

I had not expected to return alive and now the reality of my experiences were hitting me full force. I thought I was going crazy. The doctors provided me with sedatives and explained the feelings would pass. Besides, they said, I had returned somewhat in one piece and should be thankful for that. My Vietnam service was over, and while I was lucky to have survived, the nightmares continued, day and night. How long would they last? Little did I know then that they would never end.

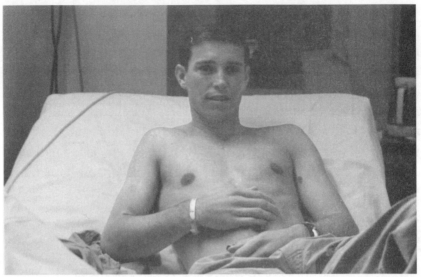

Tony in Hospital several months later   Author's Collection

A few days after being wounded I had a close call with gangrene that threatened the potential amputation of my right arm. The tourniquet applied in the field had saved my life, but cut-off blood supply to my arm and hand. The tissue was dying and infection had beset my lifeless limb. The resulting contusion had swollen my extremity to twice its normal size. Time was of the essence and the attending surgeon felt amputation was eminent. Fortunately, by some unknown fate, an unrelenting army nurse convinced the doctor to hold off until the next day. With non-stop dedication to her profession, she proceeded to massage the damaged area with hopes of detecting an element of life within. By the following morning I was able to twitch my little finger and within days I could squeeze a nutty-putty ball. I slowly regained movement throughout my hand and arm, followed by months of rehab and physical therapy. My recovery was nothing short of miraculous! The shrapnel wound to the center of my chest required the removal of a small quarter-size section of bone to extract the fragment, but somehow the sharp metal had missed my heart. I was more fortunate than many. Miracles do happen.

New recruits, of course, would follow. Most were young and innocent and unknowing about the true realities of war. For a while they would not understand the silent gaze of their battle-worn brothers, but soon enough reality would set in. Then they, too, would understand. There were more battles to fight as the horror of war raged on. Waiting for the bullet you never hear. And later, in their minds, the battles would continue long after they left the battlefield. For many, the physical and mental wounds, and resulting scars would deepen and haunt their souls for the rest of their lives.

Vietnam Wall Memorial Reflection Author's Collection

"To me the (battle) front is a mysterious whirlpool. Though I am in still water far away from its centre, I feel the whirl of the vortex sucking me slowly, irresistible, inescapably into itself."

—Erich Maria Remarque, *All Quiet On The Western Front*

Korean War Memorial   Author's Collection

Spirits from battle   Author's Collection

Understanding the War

Vietnam and troop deployment were different from most wars previous or since. Many individuals were brought in piecemeal as replacements within existing units, which made them feel disconnected from the larger group. And with no geographical lines separating friend from foe, the GI in the field could not afford to trust any locals. Villagers might be innocent civilians or Viet Cong sympathizers. Areas temporarily cleared of enemy forces could become dangerous again the next week.

It is estimated that less than a third of those who served in Vietnam actually experienced combat. Therefore, many American soldiers assigned to duty in Vietnam never witnessed large-scale battles or suffered through the terror of a jungle ambush during their one-year tours. But when they did, dozens of men could die within minutes.

Survivors often found themselves crawling over bodies trying to find somebody still alive. Often bodies had been so shot up they were unrecognizable. I remember on numerous occasions recovering a boot with foot attached or other dismembered body parts, not knowing the true identity of its owner. There was nothing left to identify. Some MIAs remain today because there was nothing left to send home. During deployment in Vietnam, the Big Red One alone suffered over 20,000 casualties. Yes, war is hell and costly.

Living in the Present

Having recently returned from a visit to the World War II battlefields in Normandy, Janet and I observed how serene, yet tragic were the thousands of seemingly endless crosses of American casualties, all of whom paid the ultimate price on foreign soil. Young men and women who charge valiantly forward into combat with all their invincibility and innocence, emerging alive or dead and forever changed.

The Spirit of Warriors   Author's Collection
Rising from the Sea at Normandy

Those who fight wars and experience combat first hand become known throughout history as warriors. Those who naively declare some hostile activity as merely a conflict have never ridden into battle and experienced the carnage, and are neither qualified nor worthy of making such assertions. Nor are they warriors.

Many who survive the horrors of combat are often afflicted with a physiological disorder, once identified as combat fatigue, but now more accurately and correctly classified as combat Post-Traumatic Stress Disorder, or PTSD. Veterans who suffer from combat PTSD, and the multitude of symptoms, do not openly share their suffering with others. Many civilians would not understand, and certainly those who never went to war are often those who least comprehend the horrors of war. This makes obvious sense, as they have never engaged in battle and have not experienced the devastation first hand.

This chapter has been about my service as a young army officer in Vietnam and how that experience changed my life forever. Unless, of course, it was all a dream, as it often seems. Actually, to be completely honest, maybe war did not change my life as I know it today. Because, in my personal reality, the call-to-duty and patriotic service during the Vietnam era does not seem to be an experience from my present lifetime. At times I remember the bravado and triumph of battles and the adrenaline thrill of charging into a victorious fight with the enemy. None of the emotions of course are rational, but then nothing about death, dying and war are rational. I do miss the rush experienced in a firefight, or the excitement of flying into battle knowing you have superior firepower and your armor is all but indestructible. But at the same time, I feel tinges of reality that help me understand I would never want to do it again.

The vague memories and horrific nightmares seem more like another time, a previous life. Maybe I have in fact been reincarnated and the person who shares my dreams of a past life is back again to work at getting it right this time. Hopefully, my karma can only get better with time. One thing I absolutely know for sure, the memories seem too removed and foreign to be a part of my present life. Only the nightmares and demons keep the experience alive and painfully real.

The demons still lurk in the dark subconscious of my mind. Is my recollection merely a dream in my world of reality or is my reality merely a dream?

My life journey with combat PTSD and finally finding the road to understanding and recovery began in the mid-1990s. I applied and was accepted to participate in a study conducted by the University of Colorado Medical Center to evaluate combat veterans who had a history of PTSD and yet performed at different levels in their readjustment to society. For the first time in my life, I found a team of medical professionals who actually understood the conditions associated with PTSD. Several members of the staff were combat veterans themselves. Following two years of extensive counseling, along with a variety of drug applications, I began to realize there was hope for living a better life.

Following the CU medical study program, I pursued ongoing treatment with the Veterans Administration, an organization I had given up on early in my life's experience. Today, I'm pleased to say the VA finally understands and is actively and openly providing help for veterans suffering from PTSD.

"My story" does not advocate a cure for PTSD, because the scars on the soul are often too deep to ever permanently heal. The scars of battle run deep in mind and body, yet the warrior's spirit is everlasting. When you have looked death in the eye and seen the destruction of humanity in living color, it invokes an element of wisdom and understanding that few comprehend. When you have met an enemy who is equally dedicated to a cause, a fundamental respect may rise that goes beyond explanation. True valor may only be fully appreciated by a fellow warrior—friend or foe.

I am hopeful that those who can relate to my story will find solace knowing that many of today's medical professionals better understand the physical and mental scars of combat—your unseen badge of courage. That simple fact alone can bring comfort. Have faith. I believe there is hope on the horizon. May you find peace as your journey continues. You have earned the right to be honored.

Photo Courtesy of U. S. Army

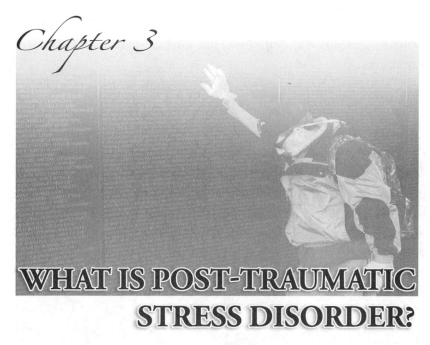

WHAT IS POST-TRAUMATIC STRESS DISORDER?

"But now, for the first time, I see you are a man like me. I thought of your hand-grenades, of your bayonet, of your rifle; now I see your wife and your face and our fellowship. Forgive me, comrade. We always see it too late. Why do they never tell us that you are poor devils like us, that your mothers are just as anxious as ours, and that we have the same fear of death, and the same dying and the same agony— Forgive me, comrade; how could you be my enemy?."

—Erich Maria Remarque, *All Quiet On The Western Front*

"A deep distress hath humanized my soul."
—William Wordsworth

"Most traumas occur on a massive scale in wars, and much of our understanding of traumatic reactions has come from those who have survived prolonged combat experience. War-related trauma is severe, repeated, and prolonged. The trauma of war comes not only from being the passive victim of violence, but also an active perpetrator. Being an active participant in the violence is also traumatic. Participating in war and becoming 'a killer' do violence to one's identity" (Allen, Jon G. *Coping With Trauma: A Guide to Self-Understanding,* American Psychiatric Press, Inc., 1995, 7-8).

John (Jan's brother) at Vietnam Memorial in Washington, D.C.

Author's Collection

History of PTSD

"It could go on for years and years, and has for centuries," wrote the author of the Sumerian epic of Gilgamesh in the third millennium, B.C., describing the sufferings of a character who survived a violent encounter that killed his friend" (Harvard Mental Health Letter, Vol. 24, 2007). Throughout history there has been documentation of how war affects the warrior. During the Civil War they called it *Irritable Heart*. During World War I and II it was referred to as *Shell Shock* and other terms described it as *Neurosis, Combat Fatigue, or Combat Exhaustion*. It is hard to imagine, but until Vietnam there was no recognition of PTSD or medical name for the disorder. Few interventions or treatments were tried with the traumatized vet. Stories from other wars, like World War I and II and even the Civil War, indicate that soldiers returning from combat faced the daunting task of trying to assimilate back into civilian life while a part of their minds and souls remained in constant torment from the battle.

In 1887, at a hospital in Paris, the Hopital du Salpetriere, a scientist by the name of Charcot and his assistant, Janet, were the first to suggest that "during traumatic events, people experience 'vehement emotions' that interfere with the integration of the overwhelming physical experience" (Bessel A. van der Kolk, *Healing Trauma,* 174). In layman's terms, the traumatic experience made it difficult for the victim to have a beginning, middle, and end to the event. The ordeal froze itself in the mind and body of the sufferer and remained hidden within the unconscious memory system. Therefore, when reminders such as an image, a smell, a physical sensation, or a sound of the original trauma occur the trauma reappears as if it was happening in real time.

Until recently, few of us knew about such a thing as Post-Traumatic stress. The veteran and his family (for most of the wars until the Gulf War, vets were mainly men) were left to make the journey through the labyrinth of behaviors and feelings on their own, with little support or understanding of the territory they were to travel. Once home, many veterans and their families were faced with the daily challenge of trying to negotiate and avoid the triggers that drew out the invisible demons: the memories and past experiences that continue to impact a vet's behavior and ability to live tranquilly in the civilian world.

On Duty   Photo Courtesy of U. S. Army, Petty Officer 1st Class Bart A. Bauer

Trauma

Trauma is a silent, invisible adversary that makes daily life a greater challenge. It is becoming an epidemic in the twenty-first century due to an increase in violence across continents. Recognizing and acknowledging trauma's impact on a person's existence is the first step to healing.

What is important to understand is that trauma changes one's life. It changes your emotional status and coping systems and impacts your physical health and well being. It influences the quality of your relationships both personal and professional. It alters how you think and process information as well as sometimes what you think, even in spite of your best effort *not* to *think* at all! It paralyzes you with numbness and uses denial, avoidance, and isolation as coping mechanisms so you don't have to deal with the memories. It impairs cognition and brain functions in ways that neuroscience is only beginning to explore and understand.

Philip Caputo, in his book *Rumor of War*, describes his emotional state upon returning from Vietnam,

> *"I hoped there would be no more surprises. I had survived enough ambushes and doubted my capacity to endure many more physical or emotional shocks. I had all the symptoms of combat veteranitis (now know as PTSD): an inability to concentrate, a childlike fear of darkness, a tendency to tire easily, chronic nightmares, an intolerance of loud noises—especially doors slamming and cars backfiring—and alternating moods of depression and rage that came over me for no apparent reason. Recovery has been less than total."*

I once asked Tony what it was like when he first returned home from combat. This was his response:

"When I returned from Vietnam my experience may not have been typical of many combat veterans who were immediately expected to get on with their lives and adjust quickly to the same homeland environment they had left. For the first six months after my return, I was primarily confined to military hospitals for physical therapy and rehabilitation from wounds sustained in combat. Most of my contact was with military personnel and other combat veterans. The protests and political unrest over the war did not become as obvious and pronounced for me until I began to interact with society and experience first hand the discontent throughout America.

Cities appeared to be far more involved and active in the war protest than what was occurring in small town America. Most of my rural family members were quite patriotic and many had served in previous wars. In general, they were supportive of my military service and appeared proud of my commitment to serve my country. When I was finally able to return to my hometown in Wyoming, many of my friends and former classmates who had never left home appeared somewhat ambivalent about the war and often acted as if nothing had changed. Their conversations and priorities were focused on high school activities and discussion seemed to center on sports wins over rival teams during our school years. They acted as if nothing had changed. In fact, for most of them, that was an accurate observation. For me, however, life had changed completely. And little did I realize, at the time, that life would never be the same again."

Roadside Bombing   Mark Sapp Collection

Rieckhoff made a similar observation, "You're in Baghdad one day, Brooklyn the next"—thrown into a society that is detached from the war and "almost entirely deaf to the issues, because only one percent of the population is directly touched by service, and life for most Americans has gone on normally" (Paul Rieckhoff, *Psychotherapy Networker*, Simon, 32). It is not easy to attend family functions, barbecues, or friends' parties, when, as a soldier, you know that halfway across the world others are being killed or are trying to survive the torments of battle. While you are having a drink at a bar, many of your comrades may be in the middle of an IED attack.

How does one ever fully recover from events that have occurred to the heart, mind, soul, spirit, and body? For us, the answer isn't one that is easy to share nor may society be prepared to hear and accept the reality.

Characteristics of PTSD

It is important to understand that most of the symptoms appear quickly without warning, invading the daily lives of the PTSD sufferer. They range from being quite subtle to overwhelming and appear without any conscious thought or personal control. It is difficult for the individual to discriminate between sensory information that is relevant, or appropriate to a current situation, and irrelevant or information frozen in a past distressing event. According to Steven Silvers, a combat veteran of Vietnam and currently the Director of the inpatient Posttraumatic Stress Disorder Program of the VA Medical Center in Pennsylvania, and Susan Rogers, "trauma resulting from combat and terrorism differs somewhat from trauma experienced by civilian events. Some of these differences include 1) the duration of exposure to the trauma, 2) likelihood of multiple traumas experienced in a short time span, 3) the trauma is man-man vs. natural disasters, accidents, or 'acts of God' and 4) the tendency of the a sufferer to be both victim and perpetrator of violence" (Silvers and Rogers, *Light in the Heart of Darkness*, 2002, 13-15).

Characteristics include:

Hyperarousal and abnormal startle responses—Irritability and/or jumpiness; constantly on guard:

Shortly after Tony and I were married, we lived in a large apartment complex. Two weeks after we moved into our new space, he went on a fishing trip while I remained home to relax and lounge around the pool. It was a warm Saturday afternoon. I was sitting by the complex pool, quietly reading a book and soaking up the sun when I heard a loud crash of bottles breaking and several piercing sounds of what appeared to be firecrackers exploding. Looking around, I saw a young man running from a poolside apartment screaming he had been shot. I followed him, seeing splatters of blood hit the concrete as he rushed down a group of stairs collapsing at the bottom. To this day, any loud noise that sounds like a gun shot or bottles breaking startle me physically and emotionally. Now think of a young soldier who has been surrounded by the traumas of combat for many months. For warriors who have viewed death and dying on a recurring basis, who have heard the bombs, blasts, and sounds of weapons firing, who have smelled blood and burning flesh, and who have held wounded and dying friends in their arms, they are primed to relive these memories. Once they return home, any similar sight, sound, smell, taste, or touch can remind them of that combat experience. If and when this occurs, the vet is whisked back to the battlefield to relive the horror. Due to his combat experience, his mind and body have been reprogrammed with the memories of battle. What may seem like nothing to someone else is incredibly unsettling for the PTSD veteran. The chronic trauma of war has placed the mind and body in a state of hyperarousal, a sensitivity and expectancy of danger even when the danger is over.

Medical Evacuation of a Wounded Soldier   Photo Courtesy of U. S. Army, Dave Melancon

Hypervigilance:

Imagine being in a car accident when someone rear ends you going 50 miles per hour. You suffer neck and mild head injuries along with other smaller aches and pains. Once you have recovered, you think you are fine. The only problem is every time you get into your car and someone is tailing you too closely you tend to get nervous and anxious. Sometimes you might even feel like jumping from your car and pouncing on the tailgater screaming at them to get off your bumper. Of course reasonable people don't do this, but you do notice that you never seemed to have this driving anxiety before the accident. Hypervigilance in a combat vet is somewhat like that only in a more intense manner. The soldier may have a need to always be in a guarded state, waiting for danger and ready to act. It takes an immense amount of energy both physical and mental to maintain such a state and one can tire pretty easily. The brain literally wears itself out by eroding the myelin sheath that surrounds the neuronal axons. It is a bit like taking a dull knife and constantly scraping away at a stick. Pretty soon the stick is whittled down to nothing, making it fragile to snap at the slightest impact.

Nightmares, insomnia, and night sweats:

The memories of war never entirely leave the warrior. They are always there, lurking in the darkness. They may stay silent for a long time, only to resurface years after the experience. Tony still has demons that confront his sleeping hours. Once these nightmares crop up, he can rarely get back to sleep. Partly because he is afraid they will reappear when he closes his eyes and dozes off. It is not uncommon for combat veterans to have chronic sleep problems and suffer from sleep deprivation. On several occasions, after a particular vivid nightmare, Tony will wake shaking and sweating profusely. He'll roll from the bed and move quietly through the dark into the bathroom, turn on the lights, and look at his hands and body. He is checking to see if he is covered with blood—either his own or the blood of his fallen comrades. It is little wonder that many veterans hate the idea of going to bed at night, yet are so tired from lack of adequate sleep they can hardly function during their waking hours.

Recurrent traumatic memories or flashbacks:

It is as if the traumatic experience is happening in current time versus in the past. The memories are vivid, the nightmares are real, and the feelings are incredibly intense. Sometimes the harder you try to forget, the more intrusive the demons. If only the bad memories would go away for good or at least diminish in intensity, perhaps one could have a greater sense of hope and some confidence that tomorrow will be better than yesterday and today.

Intrusive memories:

Have you ever tried to go on a diet and not be able to eat your favorite food, like chocolate? Seems like all you can think about is chocolate candy bars, chocolate ice cream, chocolate cake, and even chocolate milk. The harder you try not to think of chocolate, the more it appears in your mind. Darn that sweet, dark, melt in your mouth temptress. Intrusive memories are like that chocolate, only they aren't sweet. They invite themselves into your mind without a conscious invitation and stick around like an unwanted relative who won't leave after a holiday visit. If only the warrior could erase the hideous memories of battle from his psyche, perhaps life might return to some type of normal. Yet, memories are just that, memories. They don't go away. However, if the person is fortunate, over time and with skillful counseling, they may be able to dampen the intensity of the memory or at least understand and control it without becoming controlled by it. Perhaps time may give the mind a chance to adapt to the pain of the event.

Overwhelming waves of emotions *(imagine a giant tsunami in the mind and body):*

Jack be nimble, Jack be quick, Jack's an emotional lightning stick. Emotions come, emotions go, but what remains is a weary mind and soul. If only one could fully control where, when, or how hard the lightning strikes, maybe, just maybe, it could be managed. Unfortunately, emotional lightning can strike on clear days, with no clouds in the sky. It is the unpredictability of the emotions that make it so crushing.

Storm Clouds Author's Collection

Survivor guilt:

Most individuals have an innate desire to protect those they love and care about. Think of the remorse you would feel if you could not save the lives of those around you. Even though you may feel grateful that you survived, the very idea that others died or were critically wounded can gnaw on your soul. Guilt implies blame and blame carries with it a deep sense of shame and inadequacy in not fulfilling one's responsibilities or feeling capable enough to have stopped it. To live with that knowledge whether accurate or inaccurate is a heavy burden to carry through life.

Feeling detached and/or emotionally withdrawn from others:

As humans we were designed to be social beings. From the beginning of time, being a part of a group offered companionship, protection, and support with the daily chores of living. It is a very real personal need. Unfortunately, severe trauma can impact a person's ability to risk being connected to others. The combat veteran may find it difficult to be around people who have never been in battle. He knows that people do not understand the suffering associated with combat, and, as a soldier, he feels he no longer fits in with the group. He feels different. He has seen, heard, felt, tasted, and touched the sickening experience of war. The high cost of detachment and withdrawal can result in extreme loneliness, emptiness, sadness, anxiety, and depression. Being in healthy relationships demand some type of open and honest communication, sharing past, present, and future experiences. As a vet, there may be little from the combat experience you want to share with even a significant other. Combat was the warrior's private world. How do you tell someone you love that you not only saw many deaths, but may have also been the perpetrator? How do you clearly explain acts of war, whether justifiable or not? Detachment may offer the PTSD sufferer a sense of emotional safety. If you keep from getting close to another individual, you may never have to endure the agony of loss and grief again.

Fragmented sense of self and identity:

It is unimaginable for most of us, as civilians, to understand how war tears at a warrior's sense of personal identity. Most vets, like Tony, were not raised to be soldiers. They were not taught to kill in order to not be killed. While growing up in small towns or large urban communities, they were not commanded to engage in life-threatening conflicts. Most young men and women serving in combat zones were raised with some sort of religious beliefs regarding caring, kindness, and a sense of the goodness in others. War can destroy many of these beliefs and replace them with a struggle between what you once were taught, and once believed, to what you were expected and had to do to survive in combat. What the warrior saw during battle was not about goodness or kindness. Love of your fellow man was replaced with fear, destruction, and sometimes hate. And this experience, for most veterans, came at a time when they were still in their late teens or early twenties. A time when the young person was still attempting to find his/her identity. A time for personal self-discovery of who one is, who one wants to be, and who one might become. Needless to say, war greatly compromises the journey of self-identity for many young warriors. The warrior may become stronger from being in battle, and they may have to pay a very high price for this power.

The Casualties of War   Photo Courtesy of U. S. Army, Staff Sgt. Aaron Allmon II

Panic attacks:

Panic attacks are a threatening, unconscious attack on a veteran's mental state. They can occur at any time in any place without warning and are most commonly brought on by some subconscious reminder of a particular horrifying battle experience. Sweating, heightened blood pressure, increased heart rate, tensing muscles, nausea, all prepare the body for fight, flight, or freeze. For

Tony, these assaults would sometimes take place in the most mundane of environments. Several times while on a family vacation traveling from one destination to another, he would experience what seemed to be the symptoms of a heart attack. We would rush to the nearest hospital where my sons and I would sit for several hours while Tony underwent a series of tests to diagnosis what was happening to his body. Each time the diagnosis was the same, either unknown causes or stress. Thank goodness it wasn't a heart attack, yet it was obvious after a number of these occurrences that the mind was physically wrecking havoc on the body. Memories of war inhabit every cell of the body. These memories resurface for what appears to be no apparent reason. As adults, most of us understand that life can be very unpredictable. Panic attacks, unfortunately, exacerbate this sense of unpredictability for the warrior, impacting his ability to feel in control of his life. Such attacks can be confusing, physically and emotionally painful, and incredibly stressful to the PTSD sufferer and his family.

Shame:

Lewis B. Smedes explains: "The difference between guilt and shame is very clear – in theory. We feel guilty for what we do. We feel shame for what we are" (DiCiacco, *Colors of Grief,* 2008, 42). In shame, vets may feel that their combat experience changed them into something that they were once taught was wrong, immoral, and offensive. Since the world knows that war and combat involves killing, returning home may be a shameful experience for some vets.

Despair:

Depression often is a common aftermath of participating in combat. It makes the individual question his ability to navigate their present and future days. Loss of physical and/or emotional well being contribute to their feelings of loss and despair.

Lethargic or lack of motivation/interest in life, work, and family:

Melissa Charette and Stephanie Lanham describe combat trauma "as a contributing factor that leads to depression, and depression often times leads to a lack of interest in things or people you once enjoyed before combat" (*Veterans and Families' Guide To Recovering From PTSD*, 2004, 30).

Fear:

Imagine trying to go through a day where every minute is a potential opportunity for physical or emotional disasters. One never knows when the final blow will come or where it may come from. It is the inconsistency of the moment that leads to the apprehension of living fully in the moment. It is hard to maintain a sense of self-confidence when terror overcomes the mind.

Avoidance:

Avoidance is a common strategy that many PTSD veterans employ to prevent further trauma to their life. They do all they can to attempt to avoid thoughts, activities, or feelings associated with their traumatic event. For Tony, being in large groups where there isn't an obvious escape route presents a huge problem. When we go to restaurants, he must sit with his back against a wall, facing an open doorway. By doing so, he feels more in control being able to see what is coming . . . just in case. We learned never to go to movies that have a great deal of blood, gore, and violence, especially if the theme has any thing to do with warfare.

Memory and concentration problems or difficulty planning:

Severe trauma like PTSD takes over the mind's ability to pay attention to the normal, mundane proceedings in life. Combat requires intense attention to the smallest detail of battle—sight, sound, smell, taste—all alert the soldier to danger. Such intense concentration imprints the brain's neural circuitry for life. The problem with these neural superhighways is that when the vet returns to civilian life stateside, the mind stays alerted to anything that might be a warning for danger. Picture trying to pay your bills, or plan for some upcoming business meeting, when any sight, sound, or other sense may remind you of being in battle. For Tony, concentration and memory wasn't a huge problem as long as his mind was completely absorbed in his business dealings or studies. It was when he was relaxing that memory and concentration became a problem.

My brother John, also a Vietnam vet, was a different story. He was easily distracted by his surroundings, making studying, employment, and family life a great deal more grueling. What might take an ordinary person an hour to read a piece of text would take him two to three times that long. Even at that, his ability to retain the information was limited. War had taken its share of neuro networks in his brain and reorganized them in ways that made learning, planning, organization, and implementation of his plans a real challenge. Prolonged stress can actually shrink the hippocampus, an important memory area, in a developing brain.

Sadness and hopelessness about future:

Profound feelings of helplessness can occur during and after battle. Helplessness can leave a person feeling hopelessly lost, not knowing where to turn or where to go to seek support or relief. Without some type of intervention, a person may slide into deep depression feeling that life is not worth living partially because it can't be controlled in a way that is safe. Helplessness steals their sense of optimism and makes them feel that they are left without any positive options to negotiate their world.

Control issues:

A soldier who was not in control of every minute detail in combat was in danger of losing his life or the lives of those around him. There was no such thing as a small detail in combat. Everything could and eventually would become a major survival factor. It is little wonder that many veterans returning from war have an enormous problem with trying to control everything and everyone around them. Few of us who live with a vet suffering from PTSD understood this. It was never explained to us, and the veteran had little to no idea that his behavior was oppressive to others.

Anger:

Anger is an obvious behavior for most people. However, the vet may not recognize the unconscious triggers that precede his outbursts. Nor do those around him understand. The smallest situation can trigger a reaction that make living with a vet suffering from PTSD extremely challenging.

Drug and alcohol abuse:

When the memories of combat become too much to endure, many vets will resort to self-medication as a way to feel normal, numb the pain, and erase the demons if only for a little while. Alcohol and drugs for many vets are the medications of choice because they are easy to purchase once they return home and can be socially acceptable. Regrettably, these self-medications only make the situation worse by adding to the problems that the vet must already face. Drug and/or alcohol addiction merely serves as another demon the vet will have to overcome on his journey back to the world. If not caught early, drugs and alcohol can overtake the brain's dopamine receptors and make recovery nearly impossible.

Another concern can be drugs properly prescribed by physicians and therapists but not taken as directed. It is easier than one might think for an individual to obtain a prescription for an antianxiety medication along with sleep and pain killers. Taken in inappropriate doses, the vet can become addicted to these meds or overdose. The Veterans Administration strives to keep track of vets and their medications, but since most prescriptions are given to vets who are not in a hospital environment, the professionals depend on and trust the vet to be responsible when taking each medication. For a combat vet who is frequently plagued with panic attacks, depression, and bodily pain, it is a fine line between how much and when to take each medication. Addiction and overdosing just add to the demons many PTSD veterans will confront after returning home.

Self-destructive behavior:

If life no longer holds meaning or if the mind and body no longer fear death, and may even wish for it, or if hopelessness destroys a person's sense of hope, and depression swallows up the joy of living, it is easier not to be protective of one's existence. Fast driving, driving under the influence of drugs and/or alcohol, being around dangerous groups, and putting oneself in dangerous situations are all effective tactics to destroy the self. Feeling out of control of one's life, living with a sense of guilt, blame, and shame can add to the self-destructive, impulsive behavior of some veterans.

Health/physical issues including rapid heart rate and breathing, increased blood pressure, muscle tension, nausea or diarrhea, head and backaches:

There is no such thing as mind or body. They are fully integrated with each other. The mind/brain impacts the well being of the body, and the body's well being impacts the mind/brain. They are inseparable. If you would drain the entire blood supply from the body, you would not be able to sustain life since the brain needs blood for survival. The brain with all of its various emotional and cognitive systems helps control the workings of the body—temperature, heart rate, digestion ability, breathing—everything that keeps a person alive. If the body experiences severe trauma it will physically remember the sensory experience of the trauma. Not only does the brain remember, but every cell that informs the brain through our five senses holds the memory. It is no small wonder that sufferers of Posttraumatic Stress Disorder not only suffer from the mental anguish of combat, but their bodies also carry the burden. Even if the vet was not physically wounded in battle, his body will retain the trauma and it may later appear in the disguise of various physical ailments and illnesses.

Brain Facts and Functioning

 "Psychological trauma affects the brain and the rest of the nervous system. To understand traumatic reactions, you must understand your biology as well as your psychology" (Allen, Jon G. *Coping With Trauma*, 1995, 23-24).

After a traumatic experience, the brain/mind may create a new home for itself. A home that is built with different materials. A home whose walls may not be as soft, peaceful, and safe as the home prior to the experience. You may no longer be able to open your doors to the outside world, for it was the experience of the world that was traumatizing. All of your senses have been reprogrammed to other signals. Signals that were once benign now warn of danger. The senses take in information from the outside world and churn it together in new ideas, feelings, and memories. Instead of seeing a stranger as safe, you now see him as a threat. You hear a loud sound and interpret it as a risk factor. You smell certain uncooked foods and are instantly reminded of rotting flesh. Nothing is ever the same. Your new "mind" home is more like Dante's Inferno. These reprogrammed senses are part of what is known as your *implicit memory* system; a system that automatically turns on without your conscious permission. The real kicker here is that the *implicit memory* system is created by past experiences, good, bad, and ugly.

Brain Functions and Diagram
Right side of lateral view of the brain

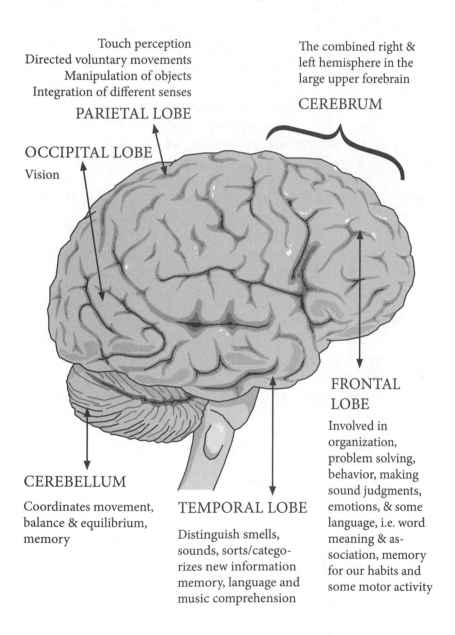

Touch perception
Directed voluntary movements
Manipulation of objects
Integration of different senses
PARIETAL LOBE

OCCIPITAL LOBE
Vision

The combined right &
left hemisphere in the
large upper forebrain
CEREBRUM

**FRONTAL
LOBE**

Involved in
organization,
problem solving,
behavior, making
sound judgments,
emotions, & some
language, i.e. word
meaning & as-
sociation, memory
for our habits and
some motor activity

CEREBELLUM

Coordinates movement,
balance & equilibrium,
memory

TEMPORAL LOBE

Distinguish smells,
sounds, sorts/catego-
rizes new information
memory, language and
music comprehension

Problems Injury/Damage Can Cause to Brain Area

BRAIN AREA	PROBLEM
Frontal Lobe	Paralysis of various parts of body, problems with memory like multiple task movements (i.e., making dinner, getting dressed), loss of flexibility in thinking, dwelling on one single thought, inability to focus on and/or complete tasks, mood and personality changes, problems interacting with others, difficulty problem solving, some language problems.
Temporal Lobe	Difficulty understanding language, recognizing faces, difficulty with attention & focusing, difficulty with speech, problems with short and long-term memory, problem categorizing objects, increased aggressive behavior, changes in sexual habit (i.e., increase or decrease).
Cerebellum	Difficulty with coordination (i.e., walking, grabbing objects), dizziness, slurred speech, shaking
Parietal Lobe	Amnesia, reading/math problems, difficulty distinguishing right/left objects, eye/hand motor coordination, lack of awareness of environment/body parts.
Occipital Lobe	Vision problems (i.e., identifying colors, seeing objects in environment), visual illusions, word blindness, difficulty reading/writing, recognizing movement, hallucinations.

PTSD and the Brain

The main and primary function of our midbrains (limbic system) is for survival. This part of our brain is always working, 24 hours a day, 7 days a week. The limbic brain (includes prefrontal cortex, anterior cingulate, hippocampus, and amygdala) along with our executive frontal cortex is an incredible organ that helps filter information in various ways to keep us safe, protect us, and help us defend ourselves when necessary. Daniel Siegel describes the brain as an "anticipation machine" derived from ongoing experience to predict what may occur in the future (*Healing Trauma: Attachment, Mind, Body, and Brain*, 2003, 26). "Its number one function is to protect its owner from danger and make survival possible. However, if a person experiences extreme stress, this can lead to neural cell death due to excessive cortisol secretion" (Siegel, 17). Cortisol and adrenaline are neurotransmitters that kick in when a person is subject to a situation that requires quick action: fight, flight, or freeze. It is part of the brain's marvelous protection, survival mechanism. Without such an amazing system it would be difficult for the human race to maintain itself.

The problem is a condition of balance. It arises, just like most of our human dilemmas, when we get too much (or too little) of something. Think of overeating. The more you eat, the more the body demands food, even unhealthy foods. A little of something is OK, even necessary and productive. A lot or too much of anything throws the body and brain out of sync and they function less efficiently. With too much additional weight, it is harder to exercise, breath, even think. Too much cortisol is a bit like having too much fat, only it's in the brain. This overabundance of cortisol actually shrinks a part of the brain know as the hippocampus. This is an area of the brain that involves short term memory—the ability to learn and retain facts. The brain is always on alert for danger, even if none is in the area. It's like a blinking red light waiting to turn green in order to allow traffic to flow through the intersection. A brain and body that is continually looking in the rearview mirror make it difficult for the driver to move forward in a safe manner. It's a challenge to focus on what is in front of you when you are engrossed in what is behind you. Stressful emotions that continually overwhelm the limbic area of the brain make it difficult to think, problem solve, and act in a rational manner. "Unresolved trauma may make entry into such states given the *proper* stressful situations more frequent, more intense, and more likely to occur with minimal provocation" (Siegel, 51).

Our senses—eyes, ears, smell, touch, taste—detect a threat and alert the brain to react by fight, flight, or freeze in order to keep us safe. Severe trauma occurs when the brain gives us a danger signal, yet we can neither fight the threat nor run from it. We are stuck. The emotions, reactions, and memories flood the system and become activated without the person ever having the sense that a traumatic memory is being recalled. It is this unconscious recollection that makes the demons so difficult to battle.

None of us knew what was happening when the mind "mines" detonated in our house. We just knew that something indiscernible happened that seem to attack our peace and make communication difficult. It is tough enough to confront an enemy when you *can* identify it; it is nearly impossible to confront one you *can't* understand. These triggers seemed to happen over and over without provocation, without warning, and without a means to defend. As a family, we all had to live with the anticipation of inner turmoil and the unpredictable personalities.

Three important factors, according to Dr. Allen make any traumatic event or stressor more difficult to cope with: "1) Unpredictability, 2) Unavoidability, and 3) Punishment of the per-

son for any efforts in trying to escape the traumatic experience."
(Allen, Jon G. Coping With Trauma, 1995, 28) "Memories can be
triggered unconsciously in just fractions of a second" (Allen, 90).

I loved the movie, *The Fisher King*, where Robin Williams
plays a mentally ill, homeless person who was once a successful
professor. His fall into hell came from the traumatic event where
his wife was killed during a shooting spree at a restaurant they
visited. Once highly functioning, his brain was unable to endure
the unspeakable. He escaped his reality by going into a state of total numbing, denial, and avoidance of anything that might evoke
a memory of his old life. My favorite line comes near the end of
the movie where he is sitting on top of a hill overlooking the city
with his new friend, Jeff Bridges, discussing the circumstances of
his life. Williams reveals his current condition stating, "my life is
this way because *'I became sick with experience.'*" An experience
that had been burned into his brain, heart, and soul and would
follow him throughout his life. An event that was so horrible that
he could not bring himself to accept reality or acknowledge the
trauma's impact on his being.

Mary Tendall and Jan Fisher explain the effects of combat
trauma in this way:

> *Because combat losses occur in a place of trauma (a com-*
> *bat zone), the brain records the event in a much different*
> *manner. Following the losses, many soldiers must oper-*
> *ate as usual, and grieving would mean letting down the*
> *emotional shield necessary for the protection of self and*
> *others. As a result of the vigilant state of the brain during*
> *the loss, the brain replays the event over and over as it is*
> *in the present.*

—www.vietnow.com, Putting Them To Rest

These repeats of traumatic events change the brain both

chemically and physically. Through these experiences the brain develops new territories, new neuro maps. What we are exposed to gets wired into our brains, our memory systems. These systems have always been there to keep us safe and ensure our survival. The memory systems allow us to learn by patterns and information from past experiences and events. Each pattern helps us discern which situations are safe, fun, pleasurable, and which may be dangerous and harmful. In other words, the brain helps us survive and navigate external events. It alerts us, informs us, and gives the rest of our bodies the appropriate cues to love, laugh, think, fight an enemy, flee, or remain frozen in place to survive.

Research on PTSD

Recent research on PTSD and its impact on the brain show how these extreme stressors actually alter the brain's chemistry and functions. The following are findings from a variety of sources on PTSD (Simon, 2005; Jankowsi, 2007; National Center for PTSD; Scaer, 2001):

- People with PTSD tend to have abnormal levels of key hormones involved in response to stress. Cortisol levels are lower than normal and epinephrine and norepinehprine (key brain neurotransmitters for fight or flight mechanisms) are higher than normal. Scientists have also found that people with this condition have alterations in the function of the thyroid and in neurotransmitter activity involving serotonin (calming and sleep chemicals in the brain/body) and opiates (pleasure & pain chemicals).

- When people are in danger they produce high levels of natural opiates, which can temporarily mask pain. Scientists have found that people with PTSD continue to produce those higher levels even after the danger is passed; this may lead to the blunted emotions (numbness, hyperarousal, hypervigilance) associated with the condition.

- Brain imaging studies indicate that the hippocampus, a part of the brain critical to emotion-laden memories, can shrink and become smaller due to the stress and trauma. Scientists are investigating whether this is related to short-term memory problems. Changes in the hippocampus are thought to be responsible for intrusive memories and flashbacks that occur in people with PTSD.

- Levels of CRF, or corticoptropin releasing factor—the ignition switch in the human stress response—seem to be elevated in people with PTSD, which may account for the tendency to be easily startled.

What does this mean?

So, what does all this neuroscience information really mean? The shortened version simply means when isolated images— smells, sights, sounds, feelings, and/or other bodily sensations arise that relate to the original trauma, it sets the body and mind into a tailspin. The person feels as if time has stopped and he is transported right back in the midst of the initial experience. There is little, if any, higher order thinking and processing going on in the frontal lobe of the brain that helps us analyze, problem-solve, and sort incoming information for meaning. At the time of the terrifying event, the mind never had the luxury to stop, think, analyze, and thoroughly process the trauma. It had to *act* fast to keep its occupant alive and safe. It is thought, therefore, that this is one underlying reason why panic attacks, flashbacks and night sweats plague the PTSD sufferer. The person literally got *stuck* in the moment. There was no time for making sense, only time for fight or flight. Because words are part of higher thinking, communication was out of the question. Who has time for words when your life is on the line? One normally does not stop to chat with a converging enemy to talk them out of being massacred. We don't pause to say, Hey, let's take a moment and think about what we are doing. That behavior would have gotten you killed. Words, appropriate sentence structure, and reasoning flew out the window with the threat.

Bessel A. van der Kolk, a noted neuroscientist explains it this way:

> *The person may feel, see, or hear the sensory elements of the traumatic experience, but he or she may be physiologically prevented from being able to translate this experience into communicable language. When they are having their traumatic recall, victims may suffer from speechless terror in which they may be literally "out of touch with their feelings."*

—Posttraumatic Stress Disorder and the Nature of Trauma, *Healing Trauma*, 2003, 187

The severity of a person suffering from PTSD can be influenced by the age when the trauma occurred (remember that in males and many females, the brain is not fully developed until the middle twenties). The intensity of the trauma, how long the trauma lasted (i.e., in combat it can be months to years), and the type of social and emotional support the person received during and after the trauma influence whether a person will later experience PTSD (van der Kolk, 179).

Statistics

Overview of PTSD Statistics

- 3.6% of U.S. adults (5.2 million Americans) have PTSD

- Women following trauma have twice the risk at developing PTSD as men (van der Kolk, *Healing Trauma*, 2003)

- 1 million Vietnam vets developed some level of PTSD after serving in the war

- 8% of Persian Gulf War vets experienced PTSD (National Mental Health Association)

- Between 20% and 30% of combat veterans and individuals exposed to high war zone stress get clinical PTSD

- Between 25% and 33% of combat vets still have PTSD today (Patience Mason, *After the War*, 1993)

- Approximately 30% of young men/women returning from Iraq and Afghanistan are experiencing some form of PTSD

Served in Vietnam 1965-1975

9,087,000 military personnel served on active duty during the Vietnam Era (August 5 1965–May 7, 1975), but only 3,403,000 served in Southeast Asia theatre (Vietnam, Laos, Cambodia, flight crews based in Thailand and sailors in adjacent South China Sea waters). (Prepared by: Washington Headquarters Services, Directorate for Information Operations and Report and Internet: http://vietnamresearch.com/history/stats.html)

Military in Southeast Asia (Men)

- 3,403,000—Deployed to Southeast Asia
- 2,594,000—Served in South Vietnam

- 1,600,000—Served in combat – approximately 1 to 1.6 million (40%-60%) either fought in combat, provided close combat support or were at least fairly regularly exposed to enemy attack

- 47,359—Hostile deaths

- 10,797—Nonhostile deaths

- 303,704—Wounded in action

- Amputations or crippling wounds to the lower extremities were 300% higher than in WWII and 70% higher than in Korea

- 25% (648,500) of total forces in country were draftees. (66% of U.S. armed forces members were drafted during WWII)

- Draftees accounted for 30.4% (17,725) of combat deaths in Vietnam

Military in Southeast Asia (Women)

- 250,000—Served in the military

- 7,484—Served in Vietnam of which 6,250 or 83.5% were nurses

- 9—Deaths

Served in Desert Shield/Desert Storm 1990-1991

- 694,550—Deployed to Gulf

- 383—Deaths

- 467—Wounded

Operation Iraqi Freedom (Iraq) – U.S. (as of May 4, 2008)

(Prepared by Defense Manpower Data Center Statistical Information Analysis Division, www.defenselink.mil/news/casualty.pdf)

- 4,067—Deaths
- 29,911—Wounded in action

Operation Enduring Freedom (Afghanistan) – U.S. (as of May 4, 2008)

(Prepared by Defense Manpower Data Center Statistical Information Analysis Division, www.defenselink.mil/news/casualty.pdf)

- 490—Deaths
- 1,936—Wounded in action

Photo Courtesy of U. S. Army, Lance Cpl. Clifton D. Sams
Woman in Combat

Characteristics of PTSD Questionnaire

Characteristics   **Since returning from combat duty:**

	Seldom True for me	Sometimes True for me	Most Often True for me
1. I am easily startled.			
2. I am easily upset.			
3. I have difficulty falling and/ or staying asleep.			
4. I often feel tense.			
5. I experience anxiety attacks at least once a week.			
6. My breathing and heart rate seem to quicken for no apparent reason.			
7. I have problems maintaining my attention when doing some tasks.			
8. I often feel depressed.			
9. I often feel disorganized when trying to complete tasks.			
10. I forget things more easily than I used to before I was in combat.			
11. I experience flashbacks during my waking and sleeping hours.			
12. I have nightmares about my combat experience.			
13. I have experienced panic attacks.			
14. I have a difficult time concentrating.			
15. I don't go to certain events or places because I am worried that I won't be able to feel comfortable being there.			
16. I engage in risky and self-destructive behavior.			

Characteristics	Since returning from combat duty:		
	Seldom True for me	Sometimes True for me	Most Often True for me
17. I use alcohol to numb my thoughts and pain.			
18. I use drugs to numb my thoughts and keep from being overly anxious.			
19. I experience sudden mood swings (i.e., anger, anxious, feelings of shame.)			
20. I often feel like I am going crazy or am out of control.			
21. I find it difficult to form close relationships with others.			
22. I feel a need to control everything in my life.			
23. I find it difficult to deal with stressful situations.			
24. I have a hard time communicating my feelings with others.			
25. I am often tired and don't have much energy to do things.			
26. I often don't feel well (i.e., headaches, stomach problems, back and/or neck problems.)			
27. I am not as interested in living my life as I was before being in combat.			
28. I often feel alone.			
29. I often feel helpless.			
30. I have a problem relaxing.			
TOTAL			

Column 1 subscore x 1 = _____

Column 2 subscore x 2 = _____

Column 3 subscore x 3 = _____

Total Score _____

> Add all three subscores to get your total score.

If you scored:

1—30 You may be experiencing normal levels of anxiety or stress.

31—60 You may be experiencing some symptoms of PTSD but these may not be severe.

61—90 You are experiencing numerous symptoms of PTSD. Please seek support and help as soon as possible.

Note:
The survey is not meant to be a clinical diagnostic tool, but an activity for readers to reflect on their current state of well being and move toward seeking support if they have not already begun the process of healing.

Chapter 4

HOW PTSD AFFECTS OTHERS

"Hundreds of thousands of women (families) are facing a silent war, one which has been fought by millions of women (families) before them."

—Patience Mason

Situation

The veteran isn't the only one affected by Post-Traumatic Stress Disorder. Spouses and families are also constantly facing odd and sometimes disturbing behavior from the vet. Often, family members become confused and wonder if something is wrong with *them* because they are emotionally affected by the actions of the vet. It is important to learn about some of the traits that vets can display and figure out ways to deal with them.

Hearing impairment can be a common trait among vets with PTSD. They can perceive the slightest noise from the farthest distance, but when it comes to listening and *hearing* those closest to them, they may seem to be hearing impaired. You can talk gently, raise your voice, or scream like a banshee, and what you get is, "I can't hear you."

The most frustrating challenge is to try and have a normal two-person conversation with someone who isn't willing or isn't able to hold a dialogue on a specific issue in an effort to understand each other. Too often, a conversation with your veteran may move into a different perspective or disagreement leading to an *all* or *nothing* event. Basic situations and discussions can get blown out of proportion. You're wrong and he must be right, for to be right for the vet is to be safe. In combat conditions, orders were vital to a mission for successful execution or potentially people died or were injured. Upon returning home, many vets have difficulty separating the combat zone from the family room.

What is going on in the mind of a veteran? Fight, flight, freeze and survival! In order for the vet to be in control of the situation, he has to have the only say. There is no time or room for an argument, disagreement, or dialogue. The prefrontal lobe is the portion of brain known as the executive thinker, the Einstein brain, the one that listens, plans, organizes, analyzes, and shuts down under trauma. And it shuts down for good reason. It is now in the territory of threat. All thinking, or lack of thinking, reverts to the limbic brain, the part of the brain in control of protecting its owner from danger. Immediate survival demands that the vet reacts in a manner that saves his and others' lives.

There is little or no time to cognitively assess or verbalize an idea or situation. As a spouse, you may recognize that you are no longer having a conversation with a thinking human being, but an uncompromising combatant.

Have you ever tried to reason with a two year old having a tantrum? If so, you may have noticed the word "reason" doesn't quite describe the situation. The only rational action is to make an effort not to debate with the person. Put distance between the parties and the discussion. Take a time out. I would love to be able to tell my vet husband *"go to your room and stay there until you can calm down!"* We used this strategy with our sons when they were young. It worked with them only because we were taller and stronger. Unfortunately, it never worked with Tony, even when *I* tried to go to *my* room to calm down.

Another idea is asking your vet to take several deep breaths before continuing the conversation. This works fine if he is not already too far into the emotional effect of the discussion. If he is emotionally overstimulated, asking him to take a few deep breaths to calm down would be similar to him making such a statement to a commanding officer right in the middle of battle.

In reality, none of this behavior was intentional or meant to be hurtful. It was, and is, a result of PTSD due to combat trauma. At the time, none of us knew about or understood PTSD. We lived in a world of perceptions and assumptions that were rarely accurate. Therefore, our problem solving was not very effective.

Often being around a vet tormented by PTSD feels like walking on egg shells. More accurately, during these emotional outbursts, life resembled trying to negotiate a field of volatile mines; never knowing where the devices resided that would trigger the explosion. Breaking a few eggs would be no big deal; being blown up emotionally was much more damaging. Holidays and family gatherings can be tenuous events at best. It is hard to have fun and be relaxed when you always have to be on guard for what might happen if the wounded warrior detonates. For the veteran and the family it is the emotional memories, the unconscious mind mines that are illusive and devastating.

Being with a person who has experienced terrible trauma definitely has a ripple effect. PTSD isn't just about the wounds of the warrior. It is about everyone around him. I have had several disagreements with mental health professionals regarding secondary PTSD. Just because there is currently no *defined* disorder within the DSM-IV (American Psychiatric Association's Diagnostic and Statistical Manual) regulations, does not mean it doesn't exist.

When living with a vet who is profoundly affected with PTSD, there can be little doubt that his behavior will not in some manner affect those around him. After a while, family members develop some of the characteristics of the trauma victim. We, too, may become anxious, overly sensitive, worried, and apprehensive of going out or being around others. We, too, may have problems with concentration and attention. Many nights we may not be able to fall asleep or wake up exhausted.

Our own sense of peace and happiness is greatly compromised. As family and friends, we want desperately to help and support the warrior. We want to heal and love him, but often times we feel alone and helpless in the battle. We may be well aware of the high price the warrior has paid for our freedom and the freedom of others. Now, we, too, pay a price for that service.

It would have helped if we could have addressed what was happening during those difficult times. But communication was challenging. The traumatized person may not feel like or even know how to share his experiences or thoughts. For the warrior, sharing these memories and emotions with others requires a great deal of courage, trust, and a tremendous amount of energy. Trust in himself that he will be strong enough to bring forth the memories consciously and without falling apart. Trust in others that they will be able to hear the stories without judging. If the experience had impacted his moral values, sharing the fear may compromise how others would now view him. He may feel ashamed and embarrassed about his combat actions. Even more difficult, the traumatized person may not even recognize or understand that his after combat actions are inappropriate and hurtful to those around him.

Many of us may not confront the warrior because we don't want to add to the hurt. Other times, we are apprehensive, afraid we might ignite his already short fuse. A lose/lose situation begins to develop—and the relationship gap grows wider.

 ### Healing Thoughts

It is essential when the "I can't hear you" pattern begins, that each individual recognizes they aren't going anywhere. Both parties may require help, a different intervention, or the use of several specific and more effective coping strategies. What isn't acceptable is to accept the vet's inappropriate behavior. The enormous stress the "I can't hear you" pattern puts on a relationship, is incredibly disruptive. At the more serious stage, it can totally destroy the love, trust, and respect necessary for a healthy rapport. The "I can't hear you" mode creates a sense of isolation and separation, not connection and caring. Distance doesn't always make the heart grow fonder.

If relationships are truly worth saving, vets and those who love them have to trust that both parties have the desire and ca-

Tony, Jan, Chad, Chris: Fishing in Alaska   Author's Collection

pacity to change to get better. It is this very faith that sets the standard for strong, enduring attachments. All of us deserve that much out of life. Expect more not less of each other. Be firm and consistent in these expectations. The expectations must be realistic. It may take outside help in order to identify the steps in a helpful manner. Remember that getting better will take lots of practice, patience and many small steps on everyone's part. Examine what is working and what isn't. Don't give up or give in. Keep trying.

And when all else fails, remember to avoid confrontation and if necessary, walk away.

You will always be given another opportunity to practice again. Walking away for a moment can reduce the stimulation that may be overwhelming for both parties at the time.

Vets sometimes shut down; go into a state of numbness and avoidance. At such a time, they may withdraw into a condition of "I can't hear anything." The inside world takes over the outside world. Humankind is just too much to deal with at that moment. In reality it may be their only way of coping. The vet needs to question what is occurring and find other ways to adjust, and those around the vet need to avoid judgment and assumptions that aren't accurate.

Another Aha!

It is quite possible that your veteran really can't hear you. Many vets, due to close proximity to explosions and loud firearms, return home with hearing problems. It is not uncommon for a person who is newly hearing impaired to nod his head, or pretend that he heard your comment. It is a coping mechanism. Hearing impairments are a frustration and can be an embarrassment to the injured party. It's one more reminder of what was damaged or lost in battle.

Going to restaurants with a great deal of surrounding noise, trying to listen to soft spoken waitresses or store attendants, or merely carrying on a normal conversation can be incredibly exhausting for someone who struggles with a hearing impairment. Tony is often annoyed when trying to order from drive-thru fast food restaurants. It is somewhat comical to observe the conversations between a metal talking box and a hearing impaired vet.

Suggestions

- If something is really important for your veteran to hear or remember **write it down**. I have found this saves a lot of aggravation and arguments, and it serves as a concrete paper trail for evidence when you need proof that information was delivered.

- Speak **directly** to the person and get **eye** contact. Most of us pay closer attention to the speaker when we are facing that person.

- Don't bother asking the person "Did you hear what I said?" Much of the time this is a waste of effort. The wounded warrior will simply nod his head and act as if everything is understood. Of course everything isn't understood, but you don't find this out until it is too late, until something you asked the person to do isn't done, or an appointment or family gathering is missed. What you believed the person heard and what is reality are very different spaces.

In the end, realize that effective communication is an absolute must for any couple or family to grow and interact in a healthy, successful manner. Few of us were ever taught or even modeled how to do this. We certainly don't have many role models on television or movies. What each person needs to appreciate is that healthy relationships take hard work and constant attention. Even in the best of situations this is not easy. When a person has been exposed to the trauma of violence stemming from combat, communication can be deeply affected. Each individual will have to work much harder to be heard and understood, as well as to be a compassionate listener. Healthy communication can be achieved with a great deal of effort, patience, and relentless practice. It is everyone's work. Don't give up.

Interesting Note:

Women be careful. We tend to talk more than males. Michael Gurian notes in his book, *Boys and Girls Learn Differently,* Jossey-Bass, 2001, 27),

Girls tend to have better verbal abilities and rely heavily on verbal communication; boys tend to rely heavily on nonverbal communication, being innately less able on average to verbalize feelings and responses as quickly as girls.

Intense communication and interactions, we can overwhelm our male significant other by too many words.

Another good reference for understanding grief and dealing with trauma can be found in the book, *The Colors of Grief: Understanding a Child's Journey through Loss from Birth to Adulthood* by Janis A. A. DiCiacco, Ph.D.

The following questionnaires are to help veterans and their spouses/families reflect on what is happening in their lives and relationships. Are things healthy and moving in the direction they want to go, or are they living with too much turmoil and conflict? The responses to the questionnaire may help give you some idea as to your present situation.

Questions
Veteran

Veterans	Give Examples	Coping Strategies
Am I as close to others as I was before serving in combat?		
When working or talking, how do I respond to those closest to me?		
Do I listen to my spouse and children without always interrupting?		
Do I speak clearly – stating my needs without blame or anger?		
What experiences do I share with my spouse or significant other? Why?		
What Experience do I not share? Why?		
Do I have trouble falling or staying asleep?		
Am I more on edge and irritable?		
Am I feeling socially isolated and alone?		
Am I easily distracted and have a difficult time concentrating?		
Am I less joyful and able to enjoy life as I was before combat?		

How may times did you answer Yes?_____ No? _____

Questions
Spouse/Family Member

Spouse/Family Member	Give Examples	Coping Strategies
Am I as close to my vet as I was before his/her combat duty?		
How does my vet respond to my needs, concerns?		
Do I listen to my vet with an open mind to understand what he/she is/has experienced?		
Do I speak clearly – stating my needs with-out blame or anger?		
How thoughtfully do I listen when my vet is sharing personal feelings and information with me?		
Do I have trouble falling and/or staying asleep?		
Am I more on edge and irritable?		
Am I feeling socially isolated and alone?		
Am I more easily dis-tracted and have a diffi-cult time concentrating?		
Am I less joyful and able to enjoy life since my vet's return from combat?		

How may times did you answer Yes?_____ No?_____

Chapter 5

KEEPING RELATIONSHIPS TOGETHER

"To keep a lamp burning we have to keep putting oil in it."

—Mother Teresa

Situation

Building and maintaining healthy, positive relationships when everything in life is going well can sometimes be difficult. Building and maintaining such a relationship when one or both parties have been traumatized from combat or other overwhelming life experiences can be a monumental challenge. Personal experiences, values, beliefs, trust, and acceptable behaviors are building blocks or barriers for any relationship. When any one of these building blocks is compromised or in conflict with one or both participants, the bond may be severely damaged. Reflecting on the many characteristics and faces of PTSD, strong relationships mean a sharing of ideas, thoughts, stories, feelings, and dreams. For the vet suffering with PTSD, sharing is not a feat he may be good at or comfortable with doing.

Many vets may find secrecy and silence more acceptable. Yet, relationships require intimacy, and intimacy involves honest and open communication. It is not that the vet may be consciously trying to conceal his past; more likely he is trying to forget it or he is trying to spare a significant other from the demons he has faced. He may feel that his demons are too horrific and perhaps too shameful to discuss. The vet is just trying to keep it together. He may feel that the demons must be kept inside, away from the civilized world of home or risk shattering what fragile stability he is trying to maintain.

So how do we keep our relationship together? The answer is both simple and complex: we keep going, day by day, hour by hour, and sometimes, minute by minute. We keep trying, struggling through the clashes, the miscommunications, the inappropriate behaviors on both our parts. We keep reading, going to counseling, and constantly striving to understand this condition called Post-Traumatic Stress Disorder. We keep praying. Praying that some of the traumatic memories will lessen in intensity, frequency, and duration. And we keep trying to love; love by recognizing the good in the other person. Love through accepting the challenge even when it feels like we are losing the battle for a healthy rapport and bond. And love in setting and adhering to suitable boundaries that keep the veteran, the spouse, and especially the children reasonably safe and protected. For example, what are some of those boundaries? No physical abuse—ever! Both parties agree to take responsibility for verbal abuse and outbursts with a genuine effort to change it. Substance abuse must be dealt with immediately, not ignored. Understanding or rationalizing unacceptable behavior is not the same as excusing the behavior.

I have not, yet, discovered or created a miraculous strategy for keeping a relationship together. There is no magic potion to staying together. It is hard and demanding work. Some days I am flabbergasted that Tony and I are still married, given the circumstances of contending with PTSD on a daily basis. Other times, I am merely humbled. Humble that we have survived. Humble that somehow, some way, we have managed to move beyond the trauma of Tony's combat wounds and my lack of knowledge and awareness of this disorder. Understanding and love are great healers.

Faith has played a huge part in our relationship. Not because we believe that couples should stay married no matter how dysfunctional the union; we don't believe this is ever a healthy option. One or more dysfunctional people do not equal a positive outcome. No, the faith we have is simply a belief in the higher good both within and beyond each of us. With this faith comes the commitment to try to do things differently.

During an especially difficult time, my twin sister, a clinical psychologist, gave me a saying that I posted on my refrigerator to read every day: Focus on what you want to have happen and then work to achieve it.

Every union of two or more individuals is different. You must decide with great honesty and clarity what it is that each of you are doing to strengthen the relationship and what you may be doing to cause the dysfunction. Sounds easy. It's not. To be honest with yourself about an unhealthy behavior takes personal candor and courage. A willingness to view yourself from a mirror that reflects all of your strengths and flaws and believe that in your humanness, you can become better, wiser, and stronger.

In the end, what you do is a choice. Yours and your vets. You either accept the challenge and move forward, or you stay in denial of the problem and/or remain in a state of hopelessness. Remember the quote by Carl Jung, "What you resist persists." Bottom line, you can move forward toward increased relational health or backward toward broken bonds and damaged hearts.

 Healing Thoughts

Suggestions for communicating with your vet from spouses and partners

Trying to communicate effectively with your vet can be a tremendous challenge. A task that can leave you feeling frustrated, angry, and even a bit crazed. Below is a list of suggestions and bits of advice to keep in mind when attempting to hold a conversation with a vet suffering from PTSD.

Choose when to communicate—especially if you have something important to discuss.

It is a waste of time to have a conversation when you or your vet is upset, angry, or in avoidance behavior. Anything you have to say will never get to the "thinking" part of the brain. In fact, your talking may only serve to overstimulate the vet's already aroused state. Pay attention to behaviors and emotions before, during, and after the conversation—yours and his. Strong emotions always trump the "thoughtful" part of the brain.

Keep what you say clear and simple.

I'm not implying that most vets aren't good listeners, but when feeling stressed they aren't. And most times, neither are many of us as significant others. Vet's minds may already be full of other thoughts and images, thus, long pieces of information may be worthless. A good rule of thumb is to evaluate what is the most critical detail you want to convey and state it clearly. Less definitely is more in this case. It may help to try to write your idea in one sentence on an index card. Doing so may cut out any unnecessary words. Sometimes, a short note will be better than a conversation, especially if emotions are volatile. I've used this on several occasions. It doesn't mean that the other party is going to be keen on reading what you have to say, but it takes away some of the personal, verbal face to face bantering.

Don't take ALL of your vet's behavior personally.

This is easier said than done especially if the conversation leads to blaming, condescension, aggression, or dodging the issues. Candidly evaluate your part of the conversation. Be sure that your own behavior and words aren't a part of an unproductive outcome. If you can honestly answer that you were specific, calm, and clear, then your partner will be more receptive to objective dialog.

Don't expect rational behavior if your vet is experiencing a panic attack, flashback, or anxiety.

The conversation isn't a conversation any longer. The reptilian, lower limbic brain has taken over. Until the episode passes anything being said will not be accurately heard or understood.

Try to communicate with metaphors and similes.

Many vets will try to describe their experiences through the use of metaphors and similes. Tony described a recent panic attack in the following way, "It was like a demon was suffocating my insides. I couldn't breathe. My heart was racing. And there seemed to be nothing I could do to stop it." Communicating in such a manner may take the emphasis off of the "me" and "I" and possibly allow the speaker to voice his thoughts without feeling too overwhelmed. It certainly gave me a pretty descriptive explanation of what Tony was going through at that moment. By listening, I gained a deeper awareness of the torment he was enduring and was more empathic to his ongoing after-combat ordeal.

It is important that you set clear and appropriate boundaries and rules for conversations and behaviors.

Setting and adhering to appropriate and clear boundaries helps keep everyone safer: the vet, the family, friends, coworkers.

Without clear limits, no one is secure. Anxiety and chaos will take over daily tasks and interactions. Without proper communication, relationships are destroyed. Trust dissolves and anger takes the place of kindness and love. Setting good boundaries can help keep communications open, productive, and safe.

Other Tidbits from the Trenches:

Try to spend more time talking about the good things. Then, when you do have to bring up a concern, it may be easier to discuss (i.e., daily activities, work related successes, children's achievements), and so forth.

Never downplay or criticize the vet for what he is feeling. Doing so can shut down communication forever and tells the vet that their experiences aren't worthy. Many vets may already feel a sense of shame and guilt. Your behaviors when listening can either add to the sorrow or ease it.

If the vet is trying to describe an experience to you; listen care-fully making eye contact, nodding your head, acknowledging you are paying attention. Don't try to change the subject. Again, doing so gives the message that the vet's experience holds no value or inter-est. This has happened countless times to Tony and made him feel quite empty and alone. You send the message that "you don't care" or "things couldn't have been that bad." To be sure, most of the time the situation was even worse than a vet could ever put into words.

*Avoid giving advice on how **you** think the vet should feel or think.* There certainly seems to be an abundance of advisors in the world with no concept of combat or war. Keep in mind that you most likely have never experienced any trauma that equals that of your vet's. You did not have to live every minute of every day for months and even years, wondering if you were going to survive the day. The average person who was born and raised in America has rarely had to endure such suffering. Hold your tongue when giving advice, unless asked for by the vet. Even then, the vet may ask for your opinion but really may only want to hear that you agree with him.

Treat the vet with respect, even if you don't understand or agree with what is being said. How the vet interprets situations may be different than yours and may be deeply impacted by his combat experiences. Trauma shocks the senses, the mind, and the heart in ways even experts don't yet fully understand.

If you are struggling with accepting or adapting to some of your vet's behaviors, you will need to address the situation im-mediately. Sooner is definitely better. Don't be naïve enough to believe that these concerns will go away the longer the vet is home. I waited thirty years and they never diminished. If only we both had some clue as to what was happening, we could have set better limits and negotiated important issues far sooner and more effectively. When stating the behavior of concern, be calm, specific and brief. If possible, always wait until both parties are calm enough to discuss behaviors that you feel need changed. This increases the likelihood that each person will be heard and successful solutions can be addressed. Trust me, this is far more difficult than anyone can imagine. I normally delayed my confrontations until my blood was boiling and couldn't wait to get in my fair share of verbal punches. Needless to say, not much was accomplished when anger was a part of the discussion.

And one last piece of advice: be careful when discussing sensitive topics such as politics, values, and religion unless you are pretty certain you know how the vet will react. Politics, value systems, and religion are hot topics that so called normal people rarely agree on. I have good friends and neighbors with whom I avoid these discussions, as we often end up feeling the other is uninformed and brainless. The big difference is you don't have to live with your neighbors or friends; you do with your vet. Irritated partners make poor house companions.

All of these suggestions and tidbits of advice may feel a bit daunting and even one-sided. In other words, if you care, you share. You share by clearly communicating how a particular behavior, not the vet, is affecting you. You share how the behavior is impacting healthy bonds. And you share how you believe in the love and capacity of the PTSD sufferer to change, to move toward well being, and to heal. Loving, sharing, communicating, and changing.

If you care, you share!

Compassion　　　　　Mark Sapp Collection

Chapter 6

SYSTEMS OF SUPPORT ON THE JOURNEY

Humpty-Dumpty sat on a wall
Humpty-Dumpty had a great fall
All the kings' horses and all the kings' men,
Couldn't put Humpty together again.

—Mother Goose Nursery Rhyme

Situation

There is a famous book and musical titled, *Stop The World, I Want To Get Off* by Leslie Bricusse and Anthony Newley that fits how Tony and

I felt. Everyone around us just keeps moving forward without near the baggage we seem to carry. They are kind, caring individuals, yet most are unaware of the trauma in our lives. Actually, most people, including some family members, may not want to know about the combat experience of the veteran. Most don't even seem to notice that Humpty Dumpty is cracked and falling apart.

If the vet or spouse tries to explain their everyday struggle, others will often change the conversation or say something incredibly sensible like: "You should just get on with your life." Even worse, they may silently think: "The story sounds a bit exaggerated." Sometimes we hear the comment that vets from World War II never seemed to suffer from PTSD. Until we became more informed about Post-Traumatic Stress Disorder, I may have been naïve enough to make a similar statement about Tony and his Vietnam experience. He was an accomplished businessman, a good father and provider, a good partner, and for the most part appeared to function just fine. Little did I understand the trauma that resided within.

Etta Shiber in her 1943 book, *Paris Underground*, described how she felt after returning home to America upon being imprisoned by the German army and almost dying for aiding British soldiers out of France:

> *The indifference I meet everywhere frightens me. I believe in human solidarity—but so many live unconcerned with the pains of their millions of brothers under the yoke! I believe in divine justice—even in our materialistic world—but I know it works through the instrumentality of human beings sufficiently in tune with it to strive for its execution. And as I see how many there are who put their own comfort above the efforts necessary to save millions of helpless beings I feel guilty myself—guilty for being here now, in a place of safety, busied with matters of no*

importance, while this clash of the forces of good and evil
is shaking the world. It is only quieting my conscience if
I say to myself that when God desires that we should act,
He shows us the way, tells us what to do—lest they die.

Veterans who have served in combat sometime suffer like this and crumble like Humpty Dumpty. After the experience—the fall—nothing can make warriors forget the event. They can be put back together but it may be weak glue that holds them somewhat intact. All it takes is one trigger to shatter the pieces. It is a constant vigilance, the need to pay attention to what those triggers are in order to gain a greater capacity of gathering and practicing strategies that help keep Humpty Dumpty together. Practicing strategies can help strengthen the glue that holds one's mind, peace, and emotions in a manageable form. A vet may never forget the pain, but the goal, like Humpty's, is that they will use the experience to grow, to become stronger; to sustain hope for the future, versus fear of the past.

Just like the mind remembers various events, the body also holds its memories through its nerve endings, muscles, and organs. The more the body's cells are stirred by a particular stimulus, the easier it is to entice those same cells to respond in the future. Think of our road system. Paths not well traveled aren't very large or effectively constructed. Those that carry large numbers of vehicles are superhighways with many lanes and faster speed options.

Your brain cells, body nerves, and muscles work the same way. They remember when they were stimulated, how many times they were stimulated, and how they responded. When a soldier is exposed to horrific warfare, his mind and body holds these memories. If this conditioning takes place before the mid-twenties when the brain is still in a developing stage, the memories and behaviors can be even more hardwired and difficult to manage once the veteran returns home. Those hardwired memories served as an effective protective device in combat allowing the vet to survive under constant threats.

So, what happens when the soldier returns home? A soldier's conditioning and memories cannot be turned on or off just by changing his environment. The soldier has been taught and practiced these drills over and over to keep him and others safe and competent in a war zone. The purpose of such training and practice is to make the actions automatic. When danger arises, the mind and body must be able to respond immediately without thinking. It is part of the fight, flight, or freeze survival mechanisms. At any point in time, each response has life and death consequences. Quick action is necessary when in combat. But back home, in the "safer" world, it is just the opposite. The normal person is encouraged to **stop** and **think** before acting. The exact opposite occurs in combat training. Unfortunately, the soldier's brain/body can't adapt its responses as efficiently. It's still running on automatic combat pilot.

One of the challenges Tony had to face when he returned from Vietnam was the adjustment to being around others who had not experienced the horrors of combat.

Most of us fortunate enough to have never experienced combat or lived in a war zone can't begin to conceive of such horrific trauma. And to be honest, we probably don't want to conjure up such unpleasant images. How easy it is for us to go on living as if everything is normal.

"Let the months and years come, they can take nothing from me, they can take nothing more. I am so alone, and so without hope that I can confront them without fear. The life that has borne me through these years is still in my hands and my eyes. Whether I have subdued it, I know not. But so long as it is there it will seek its own way out, heedless of the will that is within me."

—Erich Maria Remarque, *All Quiet On The Western Front*

Certainly, most vets feel blessed to have returned home somewhat mentally and physically intact. To the outside world they look fine. But dare to look inside and we might see a very different, disturbing picture.

Reflecting on combat - Tony Seahorn   Author's Collection

When my brother returned from Vietnam he was a different young man. He would sleep most of the day with little energy or motivation to get a job or move on with his life. Most nights he would go out and come home early in the morning feeling no pain. When he finally found work in a department store his short fuse made him less than a congenial employee. One time a couple of young hippies came into the store wearing the American flag on their butts. To a military person specifically, the flag is something quite sacred. It is the symbol of what they lived, sacrificed, and died for in combat. Seeing it worn so inappropriately was a huge trigger. Exhibiting less than a proper request for the couple to leave the store, my brother engaged in a verbal exchange about patriotism and literally escorted the two through the store entrance. Needless to say, managers of stores don't appreciate employees who toss the customer out on their rear ends.

Anger management may be a real need for some returning vets. Without the ability to manage their tempers, employment as well as healthy relationships can be difficult to keep. In addition, the stress from being angry can worsen any physical ailments they have.

Lesson for the vet: The past does impact you, but it can't destroy you unless you refuse to face it, understand it, come to terms with it, and manage the trauma. You must value the power and courage you have gained from your combat experiences. It takes guts to *see* what you really *see*. Believe that no matter what happens, you can and will come back to life. You may need to deal with the many effects of PTSD such as anger, fear, anxiety, depression, and other fallout behaviors from the combat experience. Sometimes we put ourselves in places we don't need to stay. Just because we are on a journey of healing and pass through some ugly territory, doesn't mean we have to build our house and live in that area forever.

What family and friends need to understand is PTSD is not looked at as a condition that can be cured. It is a condition that can only be managed or kept under some degree of control. So for those of us in the family support business, pray for an abundance of patience, humor, divine intervention, and perseverance.

Author's Collection

Systems of Support

Most of us would never think of climbing Mt. Everest or swimming the English Channel without establishing a competent team of trainers, coaches, and supporters to sustain our expedition. Returning home from combat is one of the biggest life trips you will ever take. Not only is Vietnam or Iraq just about as far away from America as you could travel, but psychologically it was one of the biggest journeys your mind would experience.

Who is or could be a part of your home team or posse? During the Wild West, when the good guys rode out to apprehend the bandits, they always went in a posse. Success was more likely if they were traveling in a group, all with one mission—get the outlaws. Your outlaw is much more complicated than that Wild West bandit. Your outlaw resides in the hidden cells of your mind and body and is a slippery enemy to identify.

Possible Posse Members:

- Spouse

- Parents

- Children

- Friends

- Counselor

- Doctors

- Spiritual Guide (priest, clergy, pastor)

St. James American Cemetery, France　　　　　Author's Collection

- Veterans' Associations

- Dog/Pet (no kidding)

Healing Thoughts

Every individual has her own life to live, his own burden to carry. Invisible wounds and experiences still scar the heart and soul. Silent screams and hidden wounds live in most of us and hide as unconscious and unforgettable memories.

> *"I try to believe that God doesn't give you more than one little piece of the story at once. You know the story of your life. Otherwise your heart would crack wider than you could handle. He only cracks it enough so you can still walk, like someone wearing a cast. But you've still got a crack running up your side, big enough for a sapling to grow out of. Only no one sees it. Everybody thinks you're one whole piece, and so they treat you maybe not as gentle as they would if they could see the crack."*
>
> —(Rebecca Wells, *The Ya, Ya Sisterhood*, Perennial Press, 1997)

Don't let your past experiences steal your joy, your faith in the goodness of mankind, your today or tomorrows. Each moment flutters too fast and is too precious to give into despair and hopelessness. Fight. Fight like hell. You may well be insanely sane.

We give lots of reason to not go to the unknown to do something. Don't wait. Just do it. No matter where you are in your life, if you just show up and do the work you need to do, you will succeed. The spirit is always willing and wanting to help. You are already in the boat and you may not know it. The journey is in progress. Be willing to embrace the adventure!

Author's Collection

"Peace does not dwell in outward things,
but within the soul."

—Fenelon

"We are made to persist.
That is how we find out who we are."

—Tobias Wolf

Questions

PTSD Wounded	Spouse/Partner
1. What keeps you from getting help?	1. What keeps you from getting help?
2. What kind of help do you want/need?	2. What kind of help do you want/need?
3. Who will be in your posse?	3. Who will be in your posse?
(circle of supporters)	(circle of supporters)
4. Where might you go to get this help/support?	4. Where might you go to get this help/support?
5. What steps will you take immediately to get help/support?	5. What steps will you take immediately to get help/support?

Chapter 7

STAYING AHEAD OF WHAT'S CHASING YOU

"People must grieve in order to get over an event and move on. Soldiers did not have opportunities to do this in the field or they would have died. After seeing and experiencing so much death and horror, one must become numb and/or insensitive to the situation to stay sane and keep alive."

—Patience H.C. Mason, *Recovering From the War*

Crosses at St. James American Cemetery, France   Author's Collection

Situation

Remember when your mom used to advise you that if you didn't tell the truth your nose would grow. Well, she was telling a white lie. Did you notice from a young age that your nose never grew, nor did your fingernails turn white when you told a lie? What about all the threats about not eating your spinach? I have yet to discover a kid who hated spinach that had the physical frame of a wimp.

There are a lot of myths out there like that, including the myth about some master model of a "normal" human being. Actually, I have spent an enormous amount of my life searching for this "normal" person in order to define the myth. I do have a friend who is at the top end of the normal continuum, along with several other acquaintances and family members at the far end of

Photo on page 131 courtesy of U.S. Army, Staff Sgt. Samuel Bendet the abnormal scale. My dilemma: I can't quite figure out how this normal friend got that way. She is in her eighties. Was it genetic? Years of good living? Or just sheer luck?

So what would be *normal* for the vet, and what is now *normal* for you? If you understand nothing else from this book, be aware of one haunting truth, **experiencing the horrors of combat can condemn the mind to its own psychological war.** Witnessing, smelling, hearing, touching death and carnage at close range and being in constant threat of bodily harm takes its toll on a person's mind, body, and soul. Many combat veterans state, "*I'd much rather be an amputee than psychologically injured. At least when you look at me you could see what my problem was*" (Frontline, "The Soldier's Heart" PBS Video, 2005). Emotional damage is a silent scream, crying inside—wrenching shrieks throughout the mind, heart, and spirit—yet no one but the psychologically wounded can hear the agony. The outside world ambles along unable, and at times unwilling, to hear the distress of those men and women who fought for the freedom of others. Veterans often deny that they were and are still tormented. They try hard to pretend that they are as *normal* as others see them. Yet, freedom isn't free and its costs are higher than most of us ever imagined.

If you look at the characteristics of Post-Traumatic Stress Disorder (Chapter 3), the concept of normal is frighteningly inconceivable. Perhaps, in our world today, we are creating a new definition of normal.

The New Normal

When Tony became frustrated, we often had no clue as to what was upsetting him. Things had to go perfectly. If we were going on vacation or to an event, we had better be packed and ready. No stragglers. The Boy Scout motto, "Be Prepared" was to be taken literally. No excuses! No explanations permitted.

It wasn't the big situations that would set Tony off, it was the little things; the things that couldn't be predicted or even identified by a normal person. Being in total control was incredibly vital to him. And his idea of being in control was not the same as the rest of the family. We didn't realize we were supposed to think, act, and respond as soldiers. We hadn't enlisted or been drafted into this family army. Yet, we seemed to always be on the verge of insubordination and we didn't even know it. Only the dog seemed to follow orders like a good soldier, but even the four-legged pooch had to go through some tough basic training to get there.

On one occasion, when we visited an amusement park, the boys wanted to go on a ride called the Sea Dragon. It was a huge boat-like apparatus in the shape of a Japanese dragon that swung swiftly from one end of the ride to the other, arching rapidly toward the clouds before sinking into a 180-degree fall. Whoosh! The Dragon moved swiftly to one side dropping quickly to the ground before lifting its heavy steel body upward. Whoosh! It plummeted to the ground before arching back to the other side. Much like a roller coaster, the ride was meant to help its riders lose their lunch through a loss of equilibrium and downward G-force. Looking at the thing, it initially appeared to be quite harmless, until you boarded the Dragon and it began to swing. Tony is a strong individual with an incredible physical constitution, however, during this fun amusement ride he could barely manage to stay in his seat. Not that he had much choice. He was caged behind a steel bar which prevented any escape from the beast's bowels.

Tony's skin turned pale and sweaty, his breathing quickened, and his anxiety level rocketed. At the time, we didn't recognize that the entertaining carnival adventure triggered a disturbing flashback. When he finally had his feet on solid ground he ran to the restroom and threw up. Once composed, he explained simply that the experience reminded him of flying helicopters in Vietnam and being shot down. The copter would plunge erratically to the ground hauling through the air with a similar G-force as the Dragon, before crashing violently into the earth killing most on board. We stayed a bit longer but Tony's need to go home to a familiar, safe place was more important than spending a few extra hours at the park.

It is incredibly difficult to comprehend how the body's memory system retains such memories, even if the mind can't consciously bring them forward. Trauma buries itself deep in the hidden memory system of the brain. The regions that encode all of our sensory inputs: sight, sound, smell, touch, and taste are quite precise in recording our experiences but not always on a mindful level. Past and present emotional experiences are fixed here. Any new occurrence that is similar in sight, sound, smell, touch, or taste from an earlier period, whether positive or traumatic, unconsciously alerts us to the familiar pattern.

For example, the sweet aroma of freshly-baked chocolate chip cookies may immediately remind us of a feeling of safety and belonging. The memory of when we came home from school and mom was waiting to reward our hard work and tired minds with these warm treats from the oven. On the other hand, if the memory is disturbing, like walking through a jungle of bamboo waiting to be ambushed at any moment, the sight, sound, and smell of bamboo is not going to bring a sense of peace or any feelings of safety to a person's psyche. Instead it can arouse the memories of danger, caution, and impending doom.

It wasn't until after our sons were grown and Tony began a treatment program by the Veterans' Hospital that I started to better understand his actions. I had accompanied him to a session with his doctor to get some perspective on PTSD behaviors. What his Veteran Administration therapist, Dr. Rodney Haug, explained made good sense and was quite poignant.

Dr. Haug described how difficult it was for a veteran who had been in combat for long periods of time, when life and death were constant companions. Where there was no such thing as a *small* decision because every decision that a soldier made had critical consequences, not only for himself but for all those in the unit. That every breath a vet took during combat was based on whether each choice, each detail was correct. There was no room for mistakes, even tiny ones. The explanation describes why many vets, once home, may feel an overwhelming need to be in control and control **everything** from the smallest detail to larger, more essential decisions. If he doesn't, in his mind, the consequence for everyone could be severe.

These combat experiences, day after day, month after month get loaded into the neuro network in the brain and are held throughout the various body sectors only to be reignited when a similar sense (sight, touch, sound, smell, and taste) months or years later occurs. The sound of a helicopter flying overhead can be enough to stop Tony's heart from beating. A traffic jam or person tailing too close in a car or a broken down vehicle on the side of the road can be more than a distraction for the vet. It can mean danger and trigger memories where such events warned of ambushes, bombs, and death. Women carrying babies wrapped cozily in blankets may bring memories of times when the baby was merely a disguise for a gun or bomb. Even when the immediate threat is long past, the psychological stress still exists. The memory is active and smoldered with emotion, reminding the warrior that the threat may still exist, real or imagined.

What was normal for the vet, Dr. Haug clarified, was the reactive behavior. Understanding how the brain receives and processes information from the senses, gave meaning as to why some outside stimuli may trigger unconscious and perilous situations. To change the behavior, to stay ahead of what is chasing you, would mean to change the brain. Not an easy task. Therefore, learning and practicing ways to calm one's self is a critical life skill necessary if the vet is ever able to continue to live successfully in the normal world. Doing so helps guide the brain to view the world as a safer place. With a great deal of practice and patience such calming and reconditioning exercises may help to lessen the anxiety and stress. "Every step in the right direction can lead to further steps; the challenge is to set development back on course" (Allen, Jon G., *Coping With Trauma*, 1995, 22).

In retrospect, I couldn't understand Tony's overreactions, and he couldn't or didn't choose to explain them. What I now realize is that the small annoyances of everyday life are big stuff to the vet. Putting into words the horrors of his war experience is often incomprehensible and sometimes beyond language. When a person endures severe trauma, the language area of the brain may not be as active as in normal conditions. The entire body is set to survive the experience through a fight, flight, or freeze choice.

Words aren't an essential mechanism for survival. They require thinking, when the body requires quick action. Therefore, asking someone to explain or describe the trauma or identify how he is feeling may be like asking a blind person what a room in a new house looks like when he enters. Without certain mindful resources, these tasks can be complicated to accomplish.

If I had known this tidbit of information earlier in our marriage, I might have been more patient, more supportive. Our sons may have tried harder to be on time, or at the very least, understood that Dad's behavior had more to do with his past experiences than his present moments and us.

However, in the end there is no way we could have been perfect enough to save him from his many demons. We could never have been more on time, more prepared, more quiet, more something. He was the one with the demons and he needed to acknowledge and fight them. We needed to support him and encourage him in the journey.

Patience Mason, author of *Recovering From the War: A Woman's Guide to Helping Your Vietnam Veteran, Your Family, and Yourself,* wrote, "Wives and families of veterans still fight this war alone, in our homes, untrained, ignorant of the real enemy which once had no name and wasn't supposed to exist." I was as much a part of the problem by trying to avoid the consequences of his demons.

Love can't rescue another from their ghosts. These hidden apparitions live inside the warrior's mind and heart; places outsiders can't touch but only watch as they slide between the past and the present.

As a wife and mother, I couldn't save Tony from his internal conflicts and pain. By attempting to do so, I only lost part of myself, sometimes becoming physically sick and depressed when his demons came too often, too much. I couldn't do enough, be enough, and this was not OK for a nurturer. Juggling the roles of wife, mother, career woman, sister, daughter, friend; I had too many balls in the air and they were crashing down around me. The tide was coming in and the juggler didn't know how to swim in the deep, crushing water.

Living With PTSD

Dr. Haug further analyzed that, "Living with PTSD (or someone with PTSD) is like being in high and low tide. When the tide is high, the vet is in a state of hyperarousal. Any tiny event can cause an outburst or an overreactive response. When the tide is low, the vet may be in a state of numbness and avoidance. The numbness can be an emotional defense mechanism to avoid any feelings that may seem unbearable to relive or acknowledge. The PTSD vet's life is a constant attempt to manage his feelings of being overwhelmed." The same event can trigger one or the other reaction.

The triggers and reactions are unpredictable and not black and white or 100% accurate. Every day, every event, every situation can be different, triggered by unseen, unknown implicit memory systems. Any outside sensory information may remind the vet of danger.

IED Hit Military Vehicle   Mark Sapp Collection

Many of our young vets returning from Iraq and Afghanistan are seeing their homeland worlds very differently than when they left. In Iraq, our fighting troops have to be on constant alert for car bombings, and roadside ambushes. Such hostile environments lived during months of combat, change perceptions and reactions. When these soldiers come home they may be unable to smoothly adjust back into normal life. This story is an example:

A few weeks after coming home from Iraq a young marine and his family decided to take a family outing to the mall. As they were driving down the highway, on top of one of the bridge overpasses was a car with a flat tire and a man standing by the roadside waving his hands to flag down help. The wife, seeing the stranded vehicle, asked her husband if they should stop and help, after all in their small town, it was just a person needing some roadside assistance. The vet, on the other hand, saw the situation entirely differently. Immediately upon spotting the disabled car on the side of the road, he shifted back to his military experience where every "stalled" car was an IED (Improvised Explosive Device)—a death bomb. In combat the marine was trained to immediately shoot the potential enemy and get away from the vicinity as quickly as possible.

For this soldier, who was now home, all the hidden memory systems took over, the sight, the sounds, the smell of danger. He began to sense the quickened beat of his heart and the sweat on his skin. The only sane thing the vet could do was to get angry, turn the car around in the middle of the street and head immediately for home and safety. Of course, he was unable or unwilling to explain any of these feelings to his wife. Consequently, she thought her husband was unreasonable and inconsiderate of her desires to go shopping. All he thought was he needed to get himself and his loved ones out of this potential danger and somewhere out of harm's way. Different perspectives driven by very different experiences.

Another Aha Moment

In combat situations most confrontations require immediate **action**. In civilian life, most confrontations require **inaction** (i.e., after a fender bender you pull to the side of the road and call the police or a tow truck. In combat, you disarm or shoot the enemy and get away quickly). Somehow, this automatic military **action** doesn't go over very well in Mayberry, USA, when **inaction** is in order.

Furthermore, combat trauma is different than most other types of civilian trauma since the vet's nightmare is compounded by the additional emotions of pride, courage, incredible personal sacrifice, and the honor and patriotism of fighting for and defending their county. To compound the emotional suffering, the vet must come to terms with the conditions of combat he may have to endure for the sake of personal, and more importantly, the unit's survival.

New Brain Home

After a traumatic experience, the brain/mind may create a new home for itself. A home that is built with different materials than a *normal* home. A home whose walls may not be as soft, peaceful, or safe as before the combat experience. The new walls are now jagged and cold. There is no sense of calm or safety. One finds it difficult to open the doors to a rational world. The information outside enters the doors and windows and churn together in a new way of processing. Instead of seeing a strange person as OK, you now see them as a threat. You hear a loud sound and interpret it as threat. Nothing is ever quite the same. Your new home in the mind is a dark cave filled with dread and fire like Dante's Inferno.

The traumatic environment physically changes the brain and develops new territories and neuro maps. What we are exposed to gets wired in our brains. The trauma of combat—death, fear, guilt, sorrow—can get wired into the brain as panic, depression, and unease. Erasing traumatic experiences is often impossible. Facing them—coming to terms with the past and acknowledging their impact on a person's life—can facilitate a better future. It is the vet's optimum control.

By no means is the journey easy or quick. On the contrary, it is extremely challenging and unrelenting. Disbelief and denial offer only limited protection for the psyche. They help filter terrible truths for a given time. When these defenses are down, the light of reality can bring despair and depression. Too much information unwrapped too soon can cause an uncontrollable emotional flood. The trick is to reorganize the information a piece at a time in a manner that can be dealt with and accepted. Just as a soldier should never go into a combat zone alone or without a plan, embarking on this journey without the guidance of a knowledgeable therapist and support team is unwise. Isolation can be the enemy of survival.

If Tony could have healed himself from the demons after thirty years of intense desire and effort he certainly would have succeeded. If our family could have done this instinctively we certainly would have. God knows we all made an effort, daily, yearly. It was only after skillful support and some interventions of a committed PTSD medical team and the Veterans' Administration that some relief commenced.

My recommendation to any vet and their family is **don't wait**! Amazing things do happen. Even miracles may require outside assistance. Allow others to take some of the load. Unpack those heavy bags and begin to acknowledge and deal with the behaviors and memories that drag you and your family down. You can do it. Help awaits.

Ask! Act! Trust!

Healing Thoughts

On one occasion when I attended a session with Tony and his counselor, I asked, how I could support Tony without becoming his scapegoat.

Dr. Haug responded with words that have stayed with me: "Hold in your heart that there isn't a specific answer for a veteran who suffers from PTSD. The behavior is an abnormal reaction to a situation and the content/behavior is not about you or me. It is about how the veteran is re-experiencing a traumatic event due to their combat experience. By staying calm and understanding, it will allow you to help the vet focus on what *it* is about and not react in a negative manner." Become the centered observer of your actions.

Helpful Suggestions

For the spouse and family members:

1. Seek first to understand when something out-of-sync happens.

2. Refrain from jumping to the conclusion that the veteran is *wrong,* even if his behavior is inappropriate. Since we can't walk in his shoes, at least try not to put spikes in the road.

3. Count to ten and breathe deep.

4. Try to clarify the action and identify a trigger, if possible.

5. Take a break; go to your own timeout room. It may be the best place in the house to think and reflect before going back for the next round of dialogue.

6.   Put yourself first or at least equal to everyone else. Before taking off in an airplane, the flight attendants always insist, "in case of an emergency put your oxygen mask on first before helping others." As spouses, shouldn't this analogy be put into our daily philosophy? When the world is crashing before our eyes we'd better go for the oxygen mask for ourselves first in order to save others: a long soak in the bathtub, lunch out with a friend, a walk in the woods are good soul replenishes.

7.   Create your own band of brothers/sisters. You need support as much as your warrior.

8.   Never forget the power of humor. Even if no one else understands or appreciates your levity.

9.   "If you're going to worry, don't do it. If you do it, don't worry." (Michael Nolan)

10.   "When you get to the end of your rope, tie a knot, hang on and swing." (Leo Buscaglia)

11.   Keep in mind, what you tolerate remains in your life. Know and set good boundaries.

12.   And my favorite Mother Teresa wisdom, "I know God won't give me anything I can't handle. I just wish he didn't trust me so much."

For the veteran:

1.   Count to ten and breathe deep.

2.   Self-talk:
        - What is your current state versus your combat experience?

        - What is your current reality versus your past experience?

3. Use aroma therapy—lavender, vanilla, sage, rosemary—are all calming scents.

4. Try to clarify the action and identify a trigger, if possible.

5. Admit that your fear at one time was real and important to your survival. However, if you continue to live as if you've never left the combat zone, your present and future life and relationships will mirror that experience. You will never achieve the peace and happiness you deserve and need.

6. Learn to meditate. If you desire peace of mind and heart, you will need to constantly work on helping to rewire your brain's circuits.

7. Practice relaxation and holding your tongue. Stop and think before you speak or act.

8. Put a note in your pocket with a positive statement like: I am always safe and at peace with myself and my world. Even if you're not, when you read the note, you can always imagine that you are, at least for the moment.

9. Focus on what you want to happen, and practice what it takes to achieve it, (i.e., practice patience, practice breathing deep, practice visualizing the good things in your life.

10. Try journaling for short periods of time.

Activity:

1. Write about the times you have felt most at peace, relaxed, and happy.

2. Next, write about when you have felt stressed, anxious, depressed.

3. Look over your responses. What patterns do you notice in both pieces? You may want to put these patterns into some kind of chart.

Relaxed	Stressed

4. Can you identify any of the triggers that cause you to feel stressed?

5. Can you control any of these triggers (i.e., stay away from big crowds, arrange to travel during off-peak hours of traffic)?

6. How can you plan for or do those things that help you feel more relaxed, at peace, and happy?

11. Consider such treatments as EMDR (eye movement desensitizing and reprogramming), biofeedback, and deep muscle massages.

12. Check with your Veteran's Administration therapist about new medications and treatments such as Virtual-Reality Simulations and Cognitive Processing Therapy recommended by the International Society for Traumatic Stress Studies (ISTSS) (DeAngelis, *Monitor on Psychology,* January 2008, 44).

Identifying and Holding Your Center:

Identifying *who* you are, what you want *in* your life, and what you want to *stand for* in your lifetime is what I refer to as the Core: the Center of your being.

Strength and Endurance   Author's Collection

Some people call this a person's principles. Stephen Covey refers to it as one of the *7 Habits of Highly Successful People.*

The difficulty in identifying and holding your Center lies in the details of the information. I doubt that many of us when we were in our late teens and early twenties took the time needed to sit down and think about the questions just presented. We were too busy: living, exploring, fitting in, or trying to establish an identity that would match the paradigm of our current environment and experiences. Most of this busy time, was not *Center* work. We were like the rolling stone, wherever the landscape took us is where we landed. If we really think about it, the outside world controlled us far more than our inside Center.

As stated, few young people truly know and have taken time to identify their Center, their Core beliefs and principles they currently value and want to continue to live by. Even some older individuals have forgotten or never thought about their foundational life principles. Covey states,

> *Principles are not invented by us or by society; they are the laws of the universe that pertain to human relationships and human organizations. They are part of the human condition, consciousness, and conscience. To the degree people recognize and live in harmony with such basic principles as fairness, equity, justice, integrity, honesty, and trust, they move toward either survival and stability or on the other hand, disintegration and destruction.*

—*Principal Centered Leadership*, Summit Books, 1991, 18

As human beings we have strengths that make us unique and resilient. And we have our flaws, our weaknesses. It is some of these vulnerable areas that make us fully human, more compassionate, more understanding of not only our struggles, but those of others.

The best way of staying ahead of what is chasing you is to first know *who* you are, *what* you want, and what you *stand for* in this life. Knowing and remembering this will greatly aid in containing your demons, for demons are afraid of the truth and the light it brings to the wounded. They cannot completely overcome nor overwhelm you, even though it feels at times like they are winning. Your Center will keep you grounded, safe, and remind you that you are the only one that is in real control of your mind, your body, and your life.

You decide. It is your work. You can do this. *You* are a *warrior*!

And for some humor remember:

"Masquerading as a normal person day after day is exhausting." Anonymous

Take a vacation from trying to always control your environment both internal and external.

Author's Collection

"He fell in October 1918, on a day that was so quiet and still on the whole front, that the army report confined itself to the single sentence: All quiet on the Western Front. He had fallen forward and lay on the earth as though sleeping. Turning him over one saw that he could not have suffered long; his face had an expression of calm, as though almost glad the end had come."

—Erich Maria Remarque, *All Quiet On The Western Front*

Chapter 8

WHAT DID WE LOSE AND WHEN WILL IT END?

"Veterans lost more than people in war. They lost ideals, belief in their leaders, the innate knowledge that nothing really bad can happen, Some lost hope. Some lost the ability to love or trust or care for anyone. Some become frozen in rage because they feel betrayed by their country and their communities."

—Adjusted from Patience Mason,
Recovering From the War, p. 242

Before we can talk about when and if the wounds of war and PTSD will ever end, we must first gain an understanding of what the veteran, and hence, his family lost by fighting in combat. For healing is a long and complex journey and grief work demands that the sufferer be heroic enough to acknowledge his loss; a loss that may include a physical wound and a loss that may change the individual's personal self-concept.

There isn't, nor will there be, an end to the suffering until the PTSD sufferer goes deep into his heart and soul and identifies what was both lost and gained by being a warrior. Yes, there are many gifts and they are much more available once the nightmares of combat are faced and acknowledged.

Situation

Given the trauma of combat, a veteran loses many things: their innocence, their trust in the decency of humanity, their sense of safety in a precarious world, and sometimes even the loss of self; who one was before the trauma occurred, and who one is now. In essence, combat vets lose a piece of themselves. It was stolen in battle. Many are searching for that piece (peace) they lost. They search for ways to plug the empty space, to keep themselves from draining away. To varying degrees, the traumas of war are enduring, weaving in and out of each stage of life, sometimes in the form of self-identity, sometimes resting quietly beneath other life events. Different people experience and grieve their losses in different ways, but every person must eventually come to terms with the demons, whether in a healthy or unhealthy way.

Philip Caputo in his book, *Rumor of War,* reflects:

"In battle we learned the old lessons about fear, cowardice, courage, suffering, cruelty, and comradeship. Most of all, we learned about death at an age when it is common to think

of oneself as immortal. Everyone loses that illusion eventually, but in civilian life it is lost in installments over the years. We lost it all at once and, in the span of months, passed from boyhood through manhood to a premature middle age. The knowledge of death, of the implacable limits placed on a man's existence, severed us from our youth as irrevocably as a surgeon's scissors had once severed us from the womb" (p. xv).

Final Flight Home   VA031538, David DeChant Collection, Vietnam
Archive, TTU

Military Casson of the Unknown Warrior VA031551, David DeChant Collection, Vietnam Archive, TTU

In an early '80s workshop by Ken Moses, he explained, "All loss is tied to a loss of a Dream". For many veterans theirs is now a *shattered dream.* One has to understand the nature of the dream in order to understand what has been lost. Dreams are personal to each individual. They are intensely linked to one's own enfoldment and actualization. When we lose dreams, we lose part of our original aspirations and we lose the pictures on the map of our life before the trauma.

Angela Matthews reflects upon the death of her fiancé in Vietnam, "It wasn't just the bodies that were buried, it was the dreams" (Laura Palmer, *Shrapnel in the Heart, Random House,* 1987, xiv). The dream Tony lost was his dream of making the military a career as a pilot. That was gone due to the severity of his wounds;

he would no longer qualify to fly under the military's strict flight physical requirements. How ironic that it was the military that gave him the dream and it was the military that took it away.

What some soldiers lose is their sense of well being; their sense of safety, and feelings of trust. After combat, they awake to a world of unpredictability and insanity. A part of their self-confidence and self-competence is replaced with doubt and apprehension. They return to their homes with prosthetic limbs and in wheelchairs. For some, their brains have literally been rearranged by traumatic injuries from improvised explosive devices (IEDs). Who they were before combat and who they are now can be very different people. Most civilians haven't a clue as to the sacrifice the vet has made for his family, his community or his country. And most communities don't realize the incredible sacrifice the family of these warriors have and will have to make on a daily basis. The silent wounds of the warrior and his family remain hushed.

Even if the warrior returns home without any obvious physical trauma, the greatest loss they face is the passing of innocence, hope, and peace. These are often replaced with anger, fear, chaos, despair, depression, and hopelessness. What was once normal is no longer. This is now the new normal. Jim Gray in the video, *Returning Home*, states:

> *Being a soldier was easier than being a veteran.*
> *They teach you how to be a soldier. You train to be a*
> *soldier, but when you come back home,*
> *who trains you to be an honorable veteran?*

The soldiers were taught how to fight, to rush into battle expecting hostility. The soldiers were taught how to shoot a gun, how to identify and overcome an enemy, secure an area, and dismantle the target. They were never taught how to deal with the aftermath of battle. They were never told about the price they would pay for killing and viewing death firsthand. And they were never taught how to return to civilian life as though nothing had changed.

In reality, everything has changed. Little things can feel overwhelming. You may feel out of control, vulnerable, and unable to hold your life together. You may want desperately to forget the horrible experiences, hoping to move forward rather than feeling trapped in the past. You may be continually and unexpectedly reminded of the events through flashbacks, nightmares, panic attacks, and a tirade of other triggers, reliving the terror over, and over. The past invades the present and feels as real and current as if it was happening at the very moment. You may feel cornered, crazy, and ashamed that you can't think or reason your way out of it, no matter how smart you are. You just want it all to end, to have the pain go away.

When a person loses himself, they also lose the relationships that were once attached to that self. Either these relationships are reconfigured to stay connected, or they are lost and new associations are formed. What becomes an almost certainty, if the vet and others who knew him before the trauma are open enough to admit, is that the relationship has changed. Many times people want things to be the same as they were before the ordeal. This is an unrealistic expectation. Life has been irrevocably altered, parts of the brain have been restructured, and the heart has been battered. There is no going back to what was, only accepting and acknowledging what is, and moving forward to what can be. Family, friends, and coworkers need to understand the change. If not, these supporters can become part of the problem instead of part of the solution. It is beneficial to be understanding, to be compassionate, and supportive, but make no mistake, it is detrimental to condone, excuse, or not hold individuals responsible for inappropriate and harmful behavior.

I did not know Tony before he went to Vietnam. This may have been one of our many blessings because I had no expectations built from prior experiences. Several spouses we talked with while writing the book commented on how hard it was to adjust to their vet once they returned from combat. They were expecting their significant other to be like he was before leaving for war. What they got back, many times, was quite different. It has been hard enough to negotiate our life together without having to be reminded of a *past* personality. Sometimes ignorance really is bliss. Sometimes not having to deal with shattered dreams prior to the relationship is advantageous. Nonetheless, dealing with PTSD all of the time, for the veteran and for his family is an exhausting and costly journey.

In answering the question: When will it end? Perhaps sooner than you think with adequate treatment and intense personal work. Perhaps never. For many, recovery is not a cure; it is a coming to terms with the loss, the demons, and the trauma. It is growing more knowledgeable about your condition, finding ways to cope, and growing stronger by gaining new insights and wisdom. Accept as true, you are a warrior. You are the rare person who has seen and endured unspeakable horrors and survived. You are more capable than you might think. You made it to today. You *can* make it to tomorrow!

 Healing Thoughts

The only way to move forward is to create new dreams; new life maps with new pictures and that will take work, trust and hope. "Don't let yesterday use up too much of today" (Cherokee saying). Trust that you are not only capable of achieving these new dreams but worthy of receiving them. "There is no way out, only a way forward" (Michael Hollings). At times, loss dares us to live forward, to live fully again.

Pathway to a Better Tomorrow   Author's Collection

Try to believe, even during the dark times, life is something to be cherished. Even in its pain and chaos it has its own tenderness. It is with such compassion we are reminded we are human with a mission to be truly humane. Sometimes I question, how can one overcome the traumas of life and use them to become stronger, more compassionate human beings? One answer Tony and I uncovered in our journey is to go beyond your fear, your anguish. Go beyond the uncertainty of what may lie ahead. Seek the courage, the humility, the resolve to live, to go on despite it all. It can be done. It is possible. Today and all of your tomorrows begin here, now. March forward. "Love yourself; get outside yourself and take action. Focus on the solution and be at peace" (Sioux Indian saying). Your happiness lives inside you. Find it. Create it. Live it.

Questions

Veteran	Responses
What physical wounds/effects are you experiencing?	
What psychological effects are you experiencing?	
What is most confusing for you about your condition and/or situation?	
What one behavior do you most want to focus on to improve?	
How will focusing on this behavior help you?	
Your spouse?	
Your children?	

Questions

Spouse/Family	Responses
What physical changes have you seen in your vet?	
What psychological changes have you seen in yourself?	
What is most confusing to you about the behavior of your vet?	
What one behavior can you focus on for yourself that would help you and your vet?	
How would focusing on this behavior help your vet? Yourself? Your children?	

Chapter 9

A PLACE
OF HOPE

*"Move forward in the hope of what can
be accomplished, and do not be held
back by what cannot be done."*

—Paul S. McElroy, *New Beginnings*

Life is Hard & Fragile   Author's Collection

Recently there has been a surge of news and media coverage about the lives of spouses, families, and soldiers and all of the emotions and challenge each face. The daily emotions of love; love for each other, love for country, and love for the service branch in which they selflessly serve. The feelings of loneliness, despair, confusion, fear, joy, laughter, worry, doubt, faith, and most of all, hope, all mixed together in an experience called life. A life, due to combat and long, frequent deployments away from home, produce a unique and continual set of traumas that confront the partakers on a regular basis.

One has to question how much trauma, how much pain, sorrow, and horror an individual can withstand, especially when it occurs over and over? Is there a threshold? A place from which you can't come back? If you cross that threshold, is it possible to find a way back? Not a way home, for home will never be the same. Yet, can there be a new place? A new home from which to begin to live? A place developed over time that is healthier, more liberating, and safe?

Most of us have read countless stories that give a sense of hope. Narratives from the Holocaust for example or testimonials from numerous scenes around the world where crimes against humanity past and present transpired. After years in agony, Elie Wiesel, recounts his experiences in a German Concentration Camp, he looks in a mirror and sees a corpse.

"From the depths of a mirror, a corpse was contemplating me. The look in his eyes as he gazed at me has never left me" (Elie Wiesel, *Night*, Hill and Wang, 1972, 115).

Many times when an individual survives indescribable trauma, the memories remain in the soul and are exposed as reflections in one's eyes. Eyes that will always remember the misery, the death, the evil committed, not only by the enemy, but sometimes by the victims themselves. Memories branded and embedded in every cell of the body even when the verbal memories can't be accessed. Memories that will flow through the neuro-networks of the brain deeply gouged and hollowed out by devastating torment.

Being able to maintain calm and peace on the inside, while one's outside world is muddled uncertainty, is tricky. To be honest, it isn't always one of our inner strengths. One late, autumn afternoon, I was working out of our home in Wyoming and Tony was on a walk with the dog, it began to snow. For those of you who are familiar with early mountain storms, they can be deadly if you are in the woods and aren't aware or prepared for the weather. In my case, I was nestled cozily by a fire catching up on some research articles. I noticed how wicked the weather was on the outside, yet how calm and relaxed I was sitting safely inside the house. The wind howled, snow fell in huge white flakes, and the temperature outside was around ten degrees with the wind-chill factor. It was not a good day to be outside.

As I studied the snowflakes building on the grass, I could enjoy the beauty of the storm, because I knew I was safe, warm, and comforted by the brilliance of the crackling fire. The blizzard metaphor made me consider that sometimes when our external environment is in turmoil, it is more important what is going on inside us to keep us calm and content that matters. The greatest protection and comfort from any storm is in us, yet, finding this safe place requires being still, and listening to the voices in our heart.

Weathering the storm.   Author's Collection

When you finally do venture into the storm, you never face the elements unprepared or stark naked. You first put on layers of warm clothing, like heavy socks and insulated snow boots. You cover your hands with thick mittens, your head and ears with a tight fitting hat to stay warm. Once properly dressed, you are prepared and protected to face the elements. And if you are really smart, you don't go out alone. You never want to walk by yourself in any fierce blizzard. Companionship and support are incredibly helpful. If you stumble or get a bit lost, someone will be there to help lift you up or guide you through the forest. If you feel you cannot go on, your companion can give the needed pep talk. And if you are just numb with tiredness and troubled with seemingly insurmountable problems, this person may sit beside you, if only to let you know you are not alone. Even man's best friend can be a lifesaver for support and comfort.

Perhaps we have been so conditioned to fear our outside storms that we have failed ourselves in forming an inner self of strength and confidence. Now, I silently state a personal affirmation:

Since I can't always control my outside world, I will build strength, confidence, and endurance in my inner self. I am safe as long as I am internally whole.

These are the times I'm reminded of the songs, *Amazing Grace,* and *When You Walk Through a Storm.* The lyrics, "I was lost but now I'm found", and "When you walk through a storm, hold your head up high, and don't be afraid of the dark" give me the strength I need to go on.

A Few Ending Thoughts for Spouses and Family Members

Being in a relationship with anyone is not always easy, whether a person has PTSD or appears to be relatively normal. Every couple, we suppose, has his/her own burdens. No twosome or family is spared the dilemmas of living together. Healthy, domestic relationships and interactions require a great deal of listening, compromise, giving, taking, and just plain perseverance.

We wish we could say that the journey we have traveled as a couple and family living with Posttraumatic Stress Disorder has been tranquil. We wish we could say that the setbacks are all behind us after over thirty years of marriage. It would be nice to tell you there are no longer days when we want to give up or we never lose our tempers. We wish we could share all of the many triggers that set Tony, and now me, into tantrums, but we haven't discovered them all. Or we could say we have developed effective coping strategies that serve us well on a consistent basis. We have absolutely progressed over the years through lessons learned and professional support. We have tools we use regularly. There are times however, when we totally lose sight of the fact we are well educated, calm human beings with knowledge of the brain and human development. Then we turn into the crazy woman and man who merely want all the pain to go away and peace to return. Immediately!

People that choose to live together go through cycles, some up, some down, and sometimes you aren't sure where you're going. The only wise advice we can offer after years of experience is to set reasonable boundaries that don't compromise the safety and emotional well being of the family.

As human beings, we tend to live up to our expectations. What we accept or tolerate in our families and ourselves, remain with us. It doesn't go away. There are no miracles to healthy attachments or marriages, only hard work and persistent attention to what we want and value in our lives.

If you have children, they need to be your prime concern. What you as a couple model and how, as a family, you each handle the struggles will be the role model you give your children. They will watch you and they will act like you. Children learn by imitation not by what you say, but what you do.

Children's physical and emotional safety is your first responsibility and you can't fulfill that commitment if the family environment isn't emotionally safe and respectful. Otherwise you are teaching them that an unsafe and disrespectful environment is okay.

When looking at the long-term picture of our collective relationship, and the interactions with our sons, the overall picture has been colored with many blessings. We have experienced far more joys than sorrows and an abundance of love woven with each family member's personal fortitude. It has been easier to make this PTSD journey together. We are morally stronger as a family unit than we would have been individually. We are emotionally more compassionate regarding the world and its people. And we are definitely more humble, for we have lived with and through the effects of the long-term trauma of war.

Thoughts for the Vet

What you committed for your country and the freedom of others was a tremendous sacrifice. The price may be higher than you ever expected, and the lifelong sacrifice more than anyone could possibly comprehend. Tony didn't. My brother didn't. Most warriors didn't. You may not be able to put an end to all your nightmares, panic attacks, or anxieties, but you don't have to increase the wounded-ness.

To live *forward* will take incredible will power, focus, stamina, and faith. The kind of focus, stamina, and faith you possessed every day you were in combat. If you did it then, you can do it now. Only today you are doing it for your family and yourself. You can't control everything in your home life anymore than you could control every element of combat. Yet, because of your combat experience you may need to work harder than others to manage fear, anger, anxiety, and personal expectations.

Healing PTSD

Posttraumatic Stress Disorder is not a condition that heals itself. At best, the wounded may come to understand its characteristics. Perhaps, with great effort, those who love their warriors will also come to recognize and value the tremendous challenge ahead for each of them and the enormous sacrifice that was given to serve one's country. The only practical solution is to seek help. The Veteran's Administration has far more competent therapists than they did when Tony returned from Vietnam. Remember, at that time there was no understanding of PTSD. War was something people fought; then they came home and were expected to resume their normal lives.

Our current world doesn't need more *super* heroes. What it needs are real heroes, common people demonstrating uncommon honor and truthfulness. The confidence to be strong, and sometimes vulnerable. The resilience to be determined and move forward even when giving up would be easier. The honesty of being fully human.

You do not have to go the next mile on your own. Others are waiting to help.

Ask for help.

Explain where you are at the time.

Believe.

And most of all **trust**! You can do this journey. Truly, you can. Your mind/body is like an old ship that has seen much and gone through many battles. It carries the scars and the stories. A legacy that makes your life priceless. It is tempting at times to want a bright, shiny new craft. Yet, the new ship would have no stories to tell; would not have been tested under desperate conditions. It is the old ship's wounds, its imperfections that make it special, make it one of a kind. It has been tried and proven seaworthy, weathered by the many storms of life. It has survived the worst seas and even though waterlogged, the vessel never sank. You are the symbol to the world of courage, endurance, and pride.

Your journey through the healing process changes the nightmares from a silent scream to a silent echo as the body, mind, soul, and spirit begin to mend. The trauma of combat's blood, violence, and death will always be the echoes you remember. With determination, awareness, time, and patience we heal. Perhaps not fully, but still we heal. The echo is far softer, gentler than the scream. It can be endured, even honored.

Therefore, stand tall warrior. Beyond all others your life has considerable meaning and sacredness. You are freedom. You are the pursuit of justice and honor. You are the world's hope. Make peace with your past. Find joy each today, and make new dreams for your tomorrow. Just as you were once trained to be a warrior in combat, now you must train yourself how to be that warrior in peace.

Lest we forget, freedom isn't free.

The Price of Freedom - Cheyenne VA Hospital   Author's Collection

Snapshot of U.S. Military Personnel and Their Families
Source: Defense Manpower Data Center 2003 report

Active Duty Members: 1.4 million

- 47 percent are 25 years old or younger.
- 58 percent are married and/or have children.
- 86,700 are single parents.
- 47,904 are part of a dual military couple.
- Active duty personnel have a total of 1.17 million children.
- 41 percent of those children are under 5 years old.
- 73 percent of couples and families live off base.

Reserve Members: 880,000

- 30 percent are 25 years old or younger.
- 59 percent are married and/or have children.
- 69,800 are single parents.
- 21,303 dual military couples.
- Reserve personnel have a total of 713,800 children.
- 24 percent of those children are under 5 years old.

Greer, Mark, *Monitor on Psychology,* **April 2005, 41**

Standing Guard Eternally-Tomb of the Unknowns   Author's Collection

Serving and Protecting   Photo courtesy of U. S. Army, Sgt. Jim Greenhill

Glossary

Adrenaline – A chemical in the brain (neurotransmitter) that activates when the body/brain is under stress.

AK-47 – Russian made rifle. Fires 7.62 mm round

Amygdala – The structure in the limbic part of the brain that registers positive and negative emotions such as joy, humor, fear, fight, flight or freeze. If incoming information from the senses records it as danger such as a loud noise or an unfamiliar person, the amygdale will quickly send a message to the hypothalamus to ready the body for fight, flight, or freeze.

Anxiety - An emotional response that results from a person's perception of an event that is assumed to be unsettling or negative.

ARVN – Army Republic of Vietnam. South Vietnam Allies

Attention - Those events that the mind/body focuses on based on emotional stimulation.

Autonomic Nervous System – The unconscious functions of the mind/body that gets activated through information entering from the senses. Fight, flight, freeze or safety responses are registered as involuntarily reactions to the incoming information.

C-130 – Hercules, four prop Air Force cargo and troop transport plane.

C-4 – Plastic explosives carried on field combat missions

CH-47 – Chinook, supply and troop transport helicopter.

Cortisol – A hormone in the adrenal gland released during times of stress. Helps prepare the body for flight or fight. When the body/brain has too much of this hormone for long periods of time, it can impact memory, immune system, and kill neuronal cells.

CU – University of Colorado

Dauntless – Black Lions Code Name in 1968

Dust-off – The code name for the Army Air Ambulance Medical Team used in combat to medivac casualties from the battlefield.

EMDR (Eye Movement Desensitization Reprocessing) – a treatment therapy for individuals experiencing the degenerating symptoms of trauma.

Endorphins – A peptide that helps control pain and helps with feelings of joy and pleasure. Meditation, laughter, exercise, and constructive healthy relationships help to raise this in the body.

Frontal Lobe – The last part of the brain to fully develop: Located just behind the forehead, often referred to as the "executive" lobe in charge of problem solving, organization, planning, making decisions, remembering, and assisting the brain in understanding and using new information. Also helps with controlling behavior through appropriate impulse control.

FSB – Fire Support Base

Hippocampus – A part of the limbic brain that processes new information and aids in memory. It allows a person to live in the present by learning new facts and experiences and helps retain the information until it is stored in long-term memories.

Without a functional hippocampus one cannot remember new declarative (facts) and episodic (events) memories.

Humvee – Armed forces all-purpose mobile, light tactical armored vehicle

Huey – Series of Army helicopters used in Vietnam such as Bell Iroquois & Cobra

IED – Improvised Explosive Device, often a homemade bomb

Implicit Memory – Memory contained in the various part of the body that is largely unconscious—one is not aware of the information as it comes forth in the brain/mind/body—it happens automatically without a person's conscious attention or permission.

KIA – Killed in Action

Klick – Military term used for kilometer.

Limbic System – The inner part of the brain that controls emotion (i.e., fear, pleasure, aggression). It contains the amygdala, thalamus, fornix, hypothalamus, hippocampus, and cingulated gyrus.

LRRP – (Long Range Reconnaissance Patrol) – Special, small four - to six-man teams utilized in the Vietnam War on highly dangerous special operations missions deep into enemy territory.

LZ – Landing Zone

Medivac – Medical evacuation helicopters from air mobile medical units

MIA – Missing in Action

NDP – Night Defensive Position

New Bs – New blood. Military troops new to combat.

Neurotransmitters – Chemicals released at the synapse to help information be transferred from one neuron to another.

NVA – North Vietnamese Army

POW – Prisoner of War

PRC-25 – Radio carried on soldier's back. Used during combat operations to communicate.

PTSD – An anxiety disorder that can develop after a person is exposed to a traumatic event such as military combat, rape, physical abuse, and natural disasters. Symptoms are similar to how a person felt during the initial experience: fear, anxiety, flashbacks, panic attacks, irritability, difficulty concentrating, wanting to be alone, sudden outbursts of anger.

Posse – a group of people identified as a team of supporters who have the ability and emotional stability to assist the person's journey with managing PTSD.

Perception – How a person's brain interprets incoming information from the senses both the internal and external environments. Enables the brain to respond quickly to a threat or danger.

RPG – Rocket Propelled Grenade

Sensory System – The way the body and brain receives and transfers information from the senses.

SOP – Standard Operating Procedures

Spooky – Aircraft gunship with gatling miniguns to maximize killing power

Stress – Information received from the senses that alert the body of danger. Results in feelings of tension, sense of urgency, and anxiety that cause the brain to release various hormones to prepare the body for fight or flight. Can be physical, psychological or both.

Tet – Vietnamese Lunar New Year Holiday period

Thalamus – Located in the limbic system of the inner brain. It relays incoming information from the various senses (eyes, ears, touch, taste, but not smell) to other parts of the brain for further processing.

Trauma – A violent or shocking event or personal experience that causes or is perceived to have the potential to cause bodily injury to oneself or others close to that person and can have a lifetime effect.

UW – University of Wyoming

VA – Veterans Administration

VC – Viet Cong, often referred to as Charlie by soldiers

WIA – Wounded in Action

Bibliography

Allen, Jon G. *Coping With Trauma: A Guide to Self-Understanding,* American Psychiatric Press, Inc., Washington, DC/London, England, 1995.

A Short History of PTSD: From Thermopylae to Hue Soldiers Have Always Had A Disturbing Reaction To War, Article Reprint Date, January 1991.

Brizendine, Louann; *The Female Brain,* Morgan Road Books, New York, 2006.

Brain Function Diagram, www.cbituk.org/GRAPHICS/brain.gif

Brown, Stew; Producer. Video, *Returning Home,* Department of Veteran Affairs, 2006

Bullying On Line: *Symptoms of Posttraumatic Stress Disorder,* www.bullyonline.org/stress/ptsd.httm. (accessed March 29, 2007).

Caputo, Philip. *Rumor of War,* Henry Holt & Company, New York, NY, 1977, 1996.

Cerebrum 2007: Emerging Ideas in Brain Science. Read, Cynthia A. Editor. Dana Press, New York, NY, 2007.

Charette, Melissa M., Lanham, Stephanie Laite. *Veterans and Families' Guide to Recovering From PTSD*, Purple Heart Service Foundation, Annandale, VA, 2004

Covey, Stephen R. *Principle Centered Leadership*, Summit Books New York, NY, 1991.

DeAngelis, Tori. "PTSD treatments grow in evidence, effectiveness", *Monitor on Psychology*, Vol. 39, #1, January 2008, 44-50.

DeAngelis, Tori. "Helping families cope with PTSD", *Monitor on Psychology*, Vol. 39, #1, January 2008.

DiCiacco, Janis A. Personal communication, 2005.

DiCiacco, Janis A. *The Colors of Grief: Understanding a Child's Journey through Loss from Birth to Adulthood*, Jessica Kingsley Publishers, London/Philadelphia., 2008.

Friedman, Matthew J. "Posttraumatic Stress Disorder: An Overview", US Department of Veterans Affairs, www.ncptsd.va.gov/facts/general/fs_overview.html. (accessed June 8, 2006).

Frontline. "The Soldier's Heart". PBS Video, 2005.

Greer, Mark. "A new kind of war", *Monitor on Psychology*, Vol. 36, #4, April 2005, 38-41.

Gurian, Michael. *Boys and Girls Learn Differently*, Jossey-Bass Publishers, San Francisco, CA, 2001.

Harvard Mental Health Letter. *Rethinking posttraumatic stress disorder*. Vol. 24, #2, August 2007.

Haug, Dr. Rodney. Psychologist Ft. Collins Veterans Center, Personal Communication: Wednesday, August 17, 2005.

Herbert, Claudia; Wetmore, Anne. *Overcoming Traumatic Stress: A Self-Help Guide Using Cognitive Behavioral Techniques,* New York University Press, Washington Square, N.Y., 1999.

Jankowsi, Kay. "National Center for PTSD Fact Sheet". US Department of Veterans Affairs, http://ncptsd.va.gov/ncmain/ncdocs/fact_shts/fs_physical_health.html. accessed, 6/4/08.

Jelinek, Pauline. "Number of PTSD Cases Rises", www.defenselink.mil, (accessed May 28, 2008).

King, Daniel W., King, Linda A. "Traumatic Stress in Female Veterans", U.S. Department of Veterans Affairs, www.ncptsd.va.gov/facts/veterans/fs_women_vets.html. (accessed June 8, 2006).

Levine, Peter; Frederick, Ann: *Waking the Tiger: Healing Trauma,* North Atlantic Books, Berkley, CA, 1997.

Mason, Patience H.C. *Recovering From the War: A Woman's Guide to Helping Your Vietnam Vet, Your Family, and Yourself,* Viking Press, New York, NY, 1990.

Palmer, Laura. *Shrapnel in the Heart: Letters and Remembrances from the Vietnam Veterans Memorial,* Random House, New York, NY, 1987.

PBS Video: *The Soldier's Heart,* www.pbs.org. 2005

PTSD Fact Sheet. www.athealth.com/Consumer/disorders/ptsdfacts.html, accessed 6/4/08.

Remarque, Erich Maria. *All Quiet On The Western Front,* Little Brown, Boston, MA, 1929.

Scaer, Robert. *The Body Bears the Burden,* The Haworth Medical Press, New York, NY, 2001.

Scaer, Robert. *The Trauma Spectrum,* W.W. Norton & Company, Inc., New York, NY, 2005.

Shiber, Etta, Collaboration with Anne and Paul Dupre. *Paris Underground,* New York: Charles Scribner's Sons, 1943.

Siegel, Daniel J. "An Interpersonal Neurobiology of Psychotherapy: The Developing Mind and the Resolution of Trauma." In *Healing Trauma: Attachment, Mind, Body, and Brain*, edited by Siegel, Daniel J.; Solomon, Marion F., 1-56. W.W. Norton & Company, Inc., New York, NY, 2003.

Silvers, Steven M., Rogers, Susan. *Light in the Heart of Darkness: EMDR & the Treatment of War and Terrorism Survivors.* W.W. Norton & Company, New York, NY, 2002.

Simon, Cecilia Capuzzi. "To Survive Stress, Keep it Brief." *The Dana Foundation's Brain in the News."* December 2005, Vol 12, #12, 1-2.

Simon, Cecilia Capuzzi. "Bringing the War Home." *Psychotherapy Networker*, January/February 2007, 28-37, 66.

Statistics: http://vietnamresearch.com/history/stats.html

Swhwartz, Jeffrey M. Begley, Sharon: *The Mind & the Brain: Neuroplasticity and the Power of Mental Force,* Regan Books, New York, NY, 2002.

Tendall, Mary; McKasy, Joanna. www.vietnow.com. Putting Them to Rest.

US Department of Veterans Affairs, "What is Posttraumatic Stress Disorder", www.ncptsd.va.gov/facts/gerneral/fswhatisptsd.html. (accessed June 8, 2006)

Van der Kolk, Bessel A. "Posttraumatic Stress Disorder and The Nature of Trauma." In *Healing Trauma: Attachment, Mind, Body, and Brain*, edited by Siegel, Daniel J.; Solomon, Marion F., 168-195. W.W. Norton & Company, Inc., New York, NY, 2003.

Weisel, Ellie. *Night,* Hill and Wang, New York, NY, 1972.

Wells, Rebecca. Divine Secrets of the *Ya, Ya Sisterhood,* Perennial Press, New York, NY, 1997.

Zona, Buy A. *The Soul Would Have No Rainbow if the Eyes Had No Tears and Other Native American Proverbs,* Simon & Schuster, New York, NY, 1994.

Angels of Steel

(Dedicated to the National Veterans Awareness Ride)

The angels cry when warriors die,
In distant lands where troubles lie.
Where sadness grows with each new day
and sorrow is not far away.

We fly on planes to reach this place
where death abides within its space.
There is no choice where I may fight
I only trust that it be right.

Each day I wake and say a prayer
to keep us safe and in God's care.
Yet, knowing well some will not live
and others may not soon forgive.

The wop, wop, wop of copter blades
will drop their cargo, then they fade.
Into the distant sky they fly
with lifeless bags inside do lie.

The scars remain within my soul
that haunts my mind and leaves a hole.
Where once the innocence of youth
was buried by the wrath of Zeus.

The bloody battles the heart must bear,
the mind cannot forget the terror.
But life goes on and must exist
for strength and honor to persist.

Across our country warriors ride
on bikes of steel with humbled pride,
To honor those who gave so much
and not forget the world they've touched.

The flag of glory they carry high
Through miles and miles of endless sky,
Reminding all of freedom's costs,
this hallowed message must not be lost.

And angels cry when warriors die,
In distant lands where troubles lie.
They hold the hope that peace will be
through freedom and democracy.

—*by Janet J. Seahorn, Ph.D*

Author's Bios

Tony Seahorn:

Following his tour of duty in Vietnam and subsequent physical therapy and recovery from combat wounds, Tony was informed by the Army that permanent nerve damage to his arm and shoulder would not allow him to pursue his dreams as a career aviator. After discharge from the service, Tony made a career in management with AT&T where he was able to complete his college education and went on to get an MBA. Recently retired; he and his wife Janet started their own Education Consulting and Outdoor Adventure business. Their travels take them far and wide. Following encouragement from family & friends, his most honored medals from combat are now displayed in a shadow box in their home. Some of which include two (2) Bronze Stars for heroism, two (2) Purple Hearts, Air Medal, Vietnamese Gallantry Cross, and Presidential Unit Citation. When not traveling and writing, Tony spends much of his time training two overly enthusiastic black lab retrievers, Chase & Hunter Bailey. They love to bird hunt, fly fish, and help guide the raft down-river.

Janet Seahorn:

Janet Seahorn has been a teacher, administrator, and consultant for thirty years. She currently teaches several classes on neuroscience and literacy as an adjunct professor for Regis University in Denver and Colorado State University in Fort Collins, CO. Jan has a Ph.D in Human Development and Organizational Systems. Her background includes an in-depth understanding of human development and neuroscience research as well as effective practices in organizational systems and change. She conducts numerous workshops on the neuroscience of learning and memory, the effects of "at-risk" environments (i.e., poverty) and brain development, and researched-based instructional practices.

Jan has worked with many organizations in the business and educational communities in creating and sustaining healthy, dynamic environments.

She has recently completed two books:

When Crap Happens Grow Zucchini: A book on how to live with dying and appreciate the crap

Foul Wisdom: Identifying the turkeys and eagles in your organization and your life.

Index

VA Centers

Facility	Address	State	Phone
Anchorage Vet Center	4400 Business Park Blvd, Suite B-34 Anchorage, AK 99503	AK	907-563-6966 Or 877-927-8387
Fairbanks Vet Center	540 4th Ave., Suite 100 Fairbanks, AK 99701	AK	907-456-4238 Or 877-927-8387
Kenai Vet Center Outstation	43299 Kalifornsky Beach Rd. Ste 4 Soldotna, AK 99669	AK	907-260-7640 Or 877-927-8387
Wasilla Vet Center	851 E. West Point Drive Suite 102 Wasilla, AK 99654	AK	907-376-4318 Or 907-376-4318
Birmingham Vet Center	1201 2nd Avenue South Birmingham, AL 35233	AL	205-212-3122 Or 877-927-8387
Hunstville Vet Center	415 Church Street, Bldg H, Suite 101 Huntsville, AL 35801	AL	256-539-5775 Or 877-927-8387
Mobile Vet Center	3221 Springhill Ave Bldg 2, Suite C Mobile, AL 36607	AL	251-478-5906 Or 877-927-8387
Montgomery Vet Center	4405 Atlanta Highway Montgomery, AL 36109	AL	334-273-7796 Or 877-927-8387
Fayetteville Vet Center	1416 N. College Ave. Fayetteville, AR 72703	AR	479-582-7152 Or 877-927-8387
Little Rock Vet Center	201 W. Broadway St. Suite A North Little Rock, AR 72114	AR	501-324-6395 Or 877-927-8387
American Samoa Vet Center	Ottoville Road Pago Pago, AS 96799 Mailing Address: P.O. Box 982942 Pago Pago, AS 96799	AS	684-699-3760 Or 877-927-8387
Chinle Vet Center Outstation	Navajo Route 7, Old BIA Complex-B59 Chinle, AZ 86503 Mailing Address: P.O. Box 1934 Chinle, AZ 86503	AZ	928-674-3682 Or 877-927-8387
Hopi Vet Center Outstation	P.O. Box 929, 1 Main St. Hotevilla, AZ 86030	AZ	928-734-5166 Or 877-927-8387
Lake Havasu Vet Center	1720 Mesquite Ste 101, P.O. Box 3237 Lake Havasu, AZ 86403	AZ	928-505-0394 Or 877-927-8387
Mesa Vet Center	1303 South Longmore, Suite 5 Mesa, AZ 85202	AZ	480-610-6727 Or 877-927-8387
Phoenix Vet Center	4020 N. 20th St. #110 Phoenix, AZ 85016	AZ	602-640-2981 Or 602-640-2981
Prescott Vet Center	3180 Stillwater Drive, Suite A Prescott, AZ 86305	AZ	928-778-3469 Or 877-927-8387
Tucson Vet Center	3055 N. First Avenue Tucson, AZ 85719	AZ	520-882-0333 Or 877-927-8387
West Valley Vet Center	14050 N. 83rd Avenue Suite 170 Peoria, AZ 85381	AZ	623-398-8854 Or 877-927-8387
Yuma Vet Center	1450 E. 16th St, Suite 103 Yuma, AZ 85365	AZ	928-271-8700 Or 877-927-8387

4B RCS Pacific Western Regional Office	420 Executive Court North Suite A Fairfield, CA 94534	CA	707-646-2988 Or 877-927-8387
Antelope Valley Vet Center	38925 Trade Center Drive, Suite J Palmdale, CA 93551	CA	661-267-1026 Or 877-927-8387
Bakersfield Vet Center	1110 Golden State Ave. Bakersfield, CA 93301	CA	661-323-8387 Or 877-927-8387
Chatsworth Vet Center	20946 Devonshire St, Suite 101 Chatsworth, CA 91311	CA	818-576-0201 Or 877-927-8387
Chico Vet Center	250 Cohasset Road, Suite 40 Chico, CA 95926	CA	530-899-6300 Or 877-927-8387
Chula Vista Vet Center	180 Otay Lakes Road, Suite 108 Bonita, CA 91902-2439	CA	877-618-6534 Or 877-927-8387
Citrus Heights Vet Center	5650 Sunrise Blvd., Suite 150 Citrus Heights, CA 95610	CA	916-535-0420 Or 877-927-8387
Concord Vet Center	1333 Willow Pass Road, Suite 106 Concord, CA 94520-7931	CA	925-680-4526 Or 877-927-8387
Corona Vet Center	800 Magnolia Avenue Suite 110 Corona, CA 92879	CA	951-734-0525 Or 877-927-8387
East Los Angeles Vet Center	5400 E. Olympic Blvd. Suite 140 Commerce, CA 90022	CA	323-728-9966 Or 877-927-8387
Eureka Vet Center	2830 G Street, Suite A Eureka, CA 95501	CA	707-444-8271 Or 877-927-8387
Fresno Vet Center	1320 E. Shaw Ave, Suite 125 Fresno, CA 93710	CA	559-487-5660 Or 877-927-8387
High Desert Vet Center	15095 Amargosa Rd, Suite 107 Victorville, CA 92394	CA	760-261-5925 Or 877-927-8387
Los Angeles Vet Center	1045 W. Redondo Beach Blvd. Suite 150 Gardena, CA 90247	CA	310-767-1221 Or 877-927-8387
Modesto Vet Center	1219 N. Carpenter Rd., Suite 12 Modesto, CA 95351	CA	209-569-0713 Or 877-927-8387
North Orange County Vet Center	12453 Lewis St. Suite 101 Garden Grove, CA 92840	CA	714-776-0161 Or 877-927-8387
Northbay Vet Center	6225 State Farm Drive Suite 101 Rohnert Park, CA 94928	CA	707-586-3295 Or 877-927-8387
Oakland Vet Center	2221 Martin Luther King Jr. Way Oakland, CA 94612	CA	510-763-3904 Or 877-927-8387
Peninsula Vet Center	2946 Broadway St. Redwood City, CA 94062	CA	650-299-0672 Or 877-927-8387
Sacramento Vet Center	1111 Howe Avenue Suite #390 Sacramento, CA 95825	CA	916-566-7430 Or 877-927-8387
San Bernardino Vet Center	1325 E. Cooley Drive, Suite 101 Colton, CA 92324	CA	909-801-5762 Or 877-927-8387
San Diego Vet Center	2790 Truxtun Road, Suite 130 San Diego, CA 92106	CA	858-642-1500 Or 877-927-8387
San Francisco Vet Center	505 Polk Street San Francisco, CA 94102	CA	415-441-5051 Or 877-927-8387

San Jose Vet Center	278 North 2nd St. San Jose, CA 95112	CA	408-993-0729 Or 877-927-8387
San Luis Obispo Vet Center	1070 Southwood Drive San Luis Obispo, CA 93401	CA	805-782-9101 Or 805-782-9101
San Marcos Vet Center	One Civic Center Dr., Suite 150 San Marcos, CA 92069	CA	855-898-6050 Or 877-927-8387
Santa Cruz County Vet Center	1350 41st Ave Suite 102 Capitola, CA 95010	CA	831-464-4575 Or 877-927-8387
South Orange County Vet Center	26431 Crown Valley Parkway, Suite 100 Mission Viejo, CA 92691	CA	949-348-6700 Or 877-927-8387
Temecula Vet Center	40935 County Center Drive, Suite A Temecula, CA 92591	CA	951-302-4849 Or 877-927-8387
Ventura Vet Center	790 E. Santa Clara St. Suite 100 Ventura, CA 93001	CA	805-585-1860 Or 877-927-8387
West Los Angeles Vet Center	5730 Uplander Way Suite 100 Culver City, CA 90230	CA	310-641-0326 Or 877-927-8387
4A RCS Western Mountain Regional Office	789 Sherman Street, Suite 570 Denver, CO 80203	CO	303-577-5207 Or 303-577-5205
Boulder Vet Center	4999 Pearl East Circle, Suite 106 Boulder, CO 80301	CO	303-440-7306 Or 877-927-8387
Colorado Springs Vet Center	602 South Nevada Avenue Colorado Springs, CO 80903	CO	719-471-9992 Or 877-927-8387
Denver Vet Center	7465 East First Avenue Suite B Denver, CO 80230	CO	303-326-0645 Or 877-927-8387
Fort Collins Vet Center	702 W Drake Builing C Fort Collins, CO 80526	CO	970-221-5176 Or 877-927-8387
Grand Junction Vet Center	2472 Patterson Road Unit 16 Grand Junction, CO 81505	CO	970-245-4156 Or 877-927-8387
Pueblo Vet Center	1515 Fortino Blvd., Suite 130 Pueblo, CO 81008	CO	719-583-4058 Or 877-927-8387
Danbury Vet Center	457 North Main St. Danbury, CT 06811	CT	203-790-4000 Or 877-927-8387
Hartford Vet Center	25 Elm Street, Suite A Rocky Hill, CT 06067	CT	860-563-8800 Or 877-927-8387
New Haven Vet Center	141 Captain Thomas Blvd. West Haven, CT 06516	CT	203-932-9899 Or 877-927-8387
Norwich Vet Center	2 Cliff St. Norwich, CT 06360	CT	860-887-1755 Or 877-927-8387
Washington DC Vet Center	1250 Taylor St, NW Washington, DC 20011	DC	202-726-5212 Or 877-927-8387
Sussex County Vet Center	20653 Dupont Blvd, Georgetown, DE 19947	DE	302-225-9110
Wilmington Vet Center	2710 Centerville Road, Suite 103 Wilmington, DE 19808	DE	302-994-1660 Or 877-927-8387
3A RCS Southeast Regional Office	450 Carillon Parkway, Suite 150 St. Petersburg, FL 33716	FL	727-410-9472 Or 877-927-8387
Bay County Vet Center	3109 Minnesota Ave, Suite 101 Panama City, FL 32405	FL	850-522-6102 Or 877-927-8387

Clearwater Vet Center	29259 US Hwy 19 North Clearwater, FL 33761	FL	727-549-3600 Or 877-927-8387
Clermont Vet Center	1655 East Highway 50 Clermont, FL 34711	FL	352-536-6701 Or 877-927-8387
Collier County (Naples) Vet Center	2705 Horseshoe Dr. South, #204 Naples, FL 34104	FL	239-403-2377 Or 239-403-2377
Daytona Beach Vet Center	1620 Mason Ave., Suite C Daytona Beach, FL 32117	FL	386-366-6600 Or 877-927-8387
Fort Lauderdale Vet Center	713 NE 3rd Ave. Ft. Lauderdale, FL 33304	FL	954-356-7926 Or 877-927-8387
Fort Myers Vet Center	4110 Center Pointe Drive, Unit 204 Ft. Myers, FL 33916	FL	239-652-1861 Or 877-927-8387
Gainesville Vet Center	105 NW 75th Street, Suite #2 Gainesville, FL 32607	FL	352-331-1408 Or 877-927-8387
Jacksonville Vet Center	300 East State St., Suite J Jacksonville, FL 32202	FL	904-232-3621 Or 877-927-8387
Jupiter Vet Center	6650 W. Indiantown Rd., Suite 120 Jupiter, FL 33458	FL	561-422-1220 Or 877-927-8387
Key Largo Vet Center Outstation	105662 Overseas Hwy. Key Largo, FL 33037	FL	305-451-0164 Or 877-927-8387
Melbourne Vet Center	2098 Sarno Road Melbourne, FL 32935	FL	321-254-3410 Or 877-927-8387
Miami Vet Center	8280 NW 27th St Suite 511 Miami, FL 33122	FL	305-718-3712 Or 877-927-8387
Okaloosa County Vet Center	6 11th Avenue, Suite G 1 Shalimar, FL 32579	FL	850-651-1000 Or 877-927-8387
Orlando Vet Center	5575 S. Semoran Blvd. #30 Orlando, FL 32822	FL	407-857-2800 Or 877-927-8387
Palm Beach Vet Center	4996 10th Ave North Suite 6 Greenacres, FL 33463	FL	561-422-1201 Or 877-927-8387
Pasco County Vet Center	7347 Ridge Road New Port Richey, FL 34668	FL	727-697-5176 Or 727-697-5176
Pensacola Vet Center	4504 Twin Oaks Drive Pensacola, FL 32506	FL	850-456-5886 Or 877-927-8387
Polk County Vet Center	1370 Ariana St Lakeland, FL 33803	FL	863-284-0841 Or 877-927-8387
Pompano Beach Vet Center	2300 West Sample Road, Suite 102 Pompano, FL 33073	FL	954-984-1669 Or 877-927-8387
Sarasota Vet Center	4801 Swift Rd. Suite A Sarasota, FL 34231	FL	941-927-8285 Or 877-927-8387
St. Petersburg Vet Center	6798 Crosswinds Dr. N Gaslight Square, Bldg A St. Petersburg, FL 33710	FL	727-549-3633 Or 877-927-8387
Tallahassee Vet Center	548 Bradford Road Tallahassee, FL 32303	FL	850-942-8810 Or 877-927-8387
Tampa Vet Center	Fountain Oaks Business Plaza; 3637 W. Waters Ave., Suite 600 Tampa, FL 33614	FL	813-228-2621 Or 813-228-2621

Atlanta Vet Center	1800 Phoenix Boulevard, Building 400, Suite 404 Box 55 Atlanta, GA 30349	GA	404-321-6111 X 5910 Or 877-927-8387
Lawrenceville Vet Center	930 River Centre Place Lawrenceville, GA 30043	GA	404-728-4195 Or 877-927-8387
Macon Vet Center	750 Riverside Drive Macon, GA 31201	GA	478-477-3813 Or 877-927-8387
Marietta Vet Center	40 Dodd St., Suite 700 Marietta, GA 30060	GA	404-327-4954 Or 877-927-8387
Muscogee County (Columbus) Vet Center	2601 Cross Country Drive, Condominium B-2 Suite 900 Columbus, GA 31901	GA	706-596-7170 Or 877-927-8387
Richmond County (Augusta)	2050 Walton Way, Suite 100 Augusta, GA 30904	GA	706-729-5762 Or 877-927-8387
Savannah Vet Center	321 Commercial Dr Savannah, GA 31406	GA	912-961-5800 Or 877-927-8387
Guam Vet Center	222 Chalan Santo Papa Reflection Ctr. Ste 201 Hagatna, GU 96910	GU	671-472-7160 Or 877-927-8387
Hilo Vet Center	70 Lanihuli Street Suite 102 Hilo, HI 96720	HI	808-969-3833 Or 877-927-8387
Honolulu Vet Center	1680 Kapiolani Blvd. Suite F-3 Honolulu, HI 96814	HI	808-973-8387 Or 877-927-8387
Kailua-Kona Vet Center	73-4976 Kamanu St Kailua-Kona, HI 96740	HI	808-329-0574 Or 877-927-8387
Kauai Vet Center	3-3367 Kuhio Hwy. Suite 101 Lihue, HI 96766-1061	HI	808-246-1163 Or 877-927-8387
Maui Vet Center	35 Lunalilo Street, Suite 101 Wailuku, HI 96793	HI	808-242-8557 Or 877-927-8387
Western Oahu Vet Center	885 Kamokila Boulevard, Unit 105 (10 RCS/4B-0621) Kapolei, HI 96707	HI	808-674-2414 Or 808-674-2414
Cedar Rapids Vet Center	4250 River Center Court NE, Suite D Cedar Rapids, IA 52402	IA	319-378-0016 Or 319-378-0016
Des Moines Vet Center	1821 22nd Street #115 Des Moines, IA 50266	IA	515-284-4929 Or 877-927-8387
Sioux City Vet Center	1551 Indian Hills Drive Suite 214 Sioux City, IA 51104	IA	712-255-3808 Or 877-927-8387
Boise Vet Center	2424 Bank Drive, Suite 100 Boise, ID 83705	ID	208-342-3612 Or 877-927-8387
Pocatello Vet Center	1800 Garrett Way Pocatello, ID 83201	ID	208-232-0316 Or 877-927-8387
Chicago Heights Vet Center	1010 Dixie Hwy, 2nd Floor Chicago Heights, IL 60411	IL	708-754-8885 Or 877-927-8387
Chicago Vet Center	7731 S. Halsted Street, Suite 200 Chicago, IL 60620-2412	IL	773-962-3740 Or 877-927-8387
DuPage County Vet Center	750 Shoreline Drive, Suite 150 Aurora, IL 60504	IL	630-585-1853 Or 877-927-8387
East St. Louis Vet Center	1265 N. 89th Street Suite 5 East St. Louis, IL 62203	IL	618-397-6602 Or 877-927-8387

Evanston Vet Center	1901 Howard St Evanston, IL 60202	IL	847-332-1019 Or 847-332-1019
Oak Park Vet Center	1515 South Harlem Forest Park, IL 60130	IL	708-383-3225 Or 877-927-8387
Orland Park Vet Center	8651 W.159th Street, Suite 1 Orland Park, IL 60462	IL	708-444-0561 Or 877-927-8387
Peoria Vet Center	8305 N. Allen Road, Suite 1 Peoria, IL 61615	IL	309-689-9708 Or 877-927-8387
Quad Cities Vet Center	1529 46th Avenue #6 Moline, IL 61265	IL	309-762-6955 Or 877-927-8387
Rockford Vet Center	7015 Rote Road, Suite 105 Rockford, IL 61107	IL	815-395-1276 Or 877-927-8387
Springfield, IL Vet Center	1227 S. Ninth Street Springfield, IL 62703	IL	217-492-4955 Or 877-927-8387
Evansville Vet Center	311 N. Weinbach Avenue Evansville, IN 47711	IN	812-473-5993 Or 877-927-8387
Fort Wayne Vet Center	5800 Fairfield Ave., Suite 265 Fort Wayne, IN 46807	IN	260-460-1456 Or 877-927-8387
Gary Area Vet Center	107 E. 93rd Ave Crown Point, IN 46307	IN	219-736-5633 Or 877-927-8387
Indianapolis Vet Center	8330 Naab Road, Suite 103 Indianapolis, IN 46268	IN	317-988-1600 Or 877-927-8387
South Bend Vet Center	4727 Miami Street South Bend, IN 46614	IN	574-231-8480 Or 877-927-9397
Manhattan Vet Center	205 South 4th Street, Suite B Manhattan, KS 66502	KS	785-350-4920 Or 877-927-8387
Wichita Vet Center	251 N. Water St. Wichita, KS 67202	KS	316-685-2221 X 41080 Or 316-685-2221
Lexington Vet Center	1500 Leestown Rd Suite 104 Lexington, KY 40511	KY	859-253-0717 Or 877-927-8387
Louisville Vet Center	1347 S. Third Street Louisville, KY 40208	KY	502-634-1916 Or 877-927-8387
Baton Rouge Vet Center	7850 Anselmo Lane Baton Rouge, LA 70810	LA	225-761-3140 Or 877-927-8387
New Orleans Vet Center	2200 Veterans Memorial Blvd. Suite 114 Kenner, LA 70062	LA	504-565-4977 Or 877-927-8387
Rapides Parish Vet Center	5803 Coliseum Blvd., Sute D Alexandria, LA 70303	LA	318-466-4327 Or 877-927-8387
Shreveport Vet Center	2800 Youree Dr. Bldg. 1, Suite 105 Shreveport, LA 71104	LA	318-861-1776 Or 877-927-8387
Boston Vet Center	7 Drydock Ave, Suite 2070 Boston, MA 02210-2303	MA	617-424-0665 Or 877-927-8387
Brockton Vet Center	1041L Pearl St. Brockton, MA 02301	MA	508-580-2730 Or 877-927-8387
Hyannis Vet Center	474 West Main Street Hyannis, MA 02601	MA	508-778-0124 Or 877-927-8387

Lowell Vet Center	10 George Street, Gateway Center Lowell, MA 01852	MA	978-453-1151 Or 877-927-8387
New Bedford Vet Center	73 Huttleton Ave., Unit 2 Fairhaven, MA 02719	MA	508-999-6920 Or 877-927-8387
Springfield Vet Center	95 Ashley Avenue, Suite A West Springfield, MA 01089	MA	413-737-5167 Or 413-737-5167
Worcester Vet Center	691 Grafton Street Worcester, MA 01604	MA	508-753-7902 Or 877-927-8387
1B RCS Mid-Atlantic Region	305 W. Chesapeake Ave., Suite 300 Towson, MD 21204	MD	410-828-6619 Or 877-927-8387
Aberdeen Vet Center Outstation	223 W. Bel Air Avenue Aberdeen, MD 21001	MD	410-272-6771 Or 877-927-8387
Annapolis Vet Center	100 Annapolis Street, Suite 102 Annapolis, MD 21401	MD	410-605-7826 Or 877-927-8387
Baltimore County - Dundalk Vet Center	1553 Merritt Blvd Dundalk, MD 21222	MD	410-282-6144 Or 877-927-8387
Baltimore Vet Center	1777 Reisterstown Road Suite 199 Baltimore, MD 21208	MD	410-764-9400 Or 877-927-8387
Cambridge Vet Center Outstation	830 Chesapeake Drive Cambridge, MD 21613	MD	410-228-6305 Or 877-927-8387
Elkton Vet Center	103 Chesapeake Blvd. Suite A Elkton, MD 21921	MD	410-392-4485 Or 877-927-8387
Prince George County Vet Center	7905 Malcolm Road, Suite 101 Clinton, MD 20735	MD	301-856-7173 Or 301-856-7173
Silver Spring Vet Center	2900 Linden Lane, Suite 100 Silver Spring, MD 20910	MD	301-589-1073 Or 877-927-8387
Bangor Vet Center	368 Harlow St. In-Town Plaza Bangor, ME 04401	ME	207-947-3391 Or 877-927-8387
Caribou Vet Center	456 York Street York Street Complex Caribou, ME 04736	ME	207-496-3900 Or 877-927-8387
Lewiston Vet Center	35 Westminster St. Lewiston, ME 04240	ME	207-783-0068 Or 207-783-0068
Portland Vet Center	475 Stevens Ave. Portland, ME 04103	ME	207-780-3584 Or 877-927-8387
Sanford Vet Center	628 Main Street Springvale, ME 04083	ME	207-490-1513 Or 877-927-8387
Dearborn Vet Center	19855 Outer Drive, Suite 105 W Dearborn, MI 48124	MI	313-277-1428 Or 877-927-8387
Detroit Vet Center	4161 Cass Avenue Detroit, MI 48201	MI	313-576-1514 Or 877-927-8387
Escanaba Vet Center	3500 Ludington Street, Suite # 110 Escanaba, MI 49829	MI	906-233-0244
Grand Rapids Vet Center	2050 Breton Rd SE Grand Rapids, MI 49546	MI	616-285-5795 Or 877-927-8387
Macomb County Vet Center	42621 Garfield Rd. Suite 105 Clinton Township, MI 48038-5031	MI	586-412-0107 Or 877-927-8387

Pontiac Vet Center	44200 Woodward Avenue, Suite 108 Pontiac, MI 48341	MI	248-874-1015 Or 877-927-8387
Saginaw Vet Center	5360 Hampton Place Saginaw, MI 48604	MI	989-321-4650 Or 989-321-4650
Traverse City Vet Center	3766 N US 31 South Traverse City, MI 49684	MI	231-935-0051 Or 877-927-8387
Brooklyn Park Vet Center	7001 78th Avenue North, Suite 300 Brooklyn Park, MN 55445	MN	763-503-2220 Or 877-927-8387
Duluth Vet Center	405 E. Superior Street, Suite 160 Duluth, MN 55802	MN	218-722-8654 Or 877-927-8387
St. Paul Vet Center	550 County Road D, Suite 10 New Brighton, MN 55112	MN	651-644-4022 Or 877-927-8387
2 RCS Central Regional Office	2122 Kratky Rd. St. Louis, MO 63114	MO	314-426-5460 Or 877-927-8387
Columbia Vet Center	4040 Rangeline Street, Suite 105 Columbia, MO 65202	MO	573-814-6206 Or 573-814-6206
Kansas City Vet Center	4800 Main Street, Suite 107 Kansas City, MO 64111	MO	816-753-1866 Or 877-927-8387
Springfield, MO Vet Center	3616 S. Campbell Springfield, MO 65807	MO	417-881-4197 Or 877-927-8387
St. Louis Vet Center	2901 Olive St. Louis, MO 63103	MO	314-531-5355 Or 877-927-8387
Biloxi Vet Center	288 Veterans Ave Biloxi, MS 39531	MS	228-388-9938 Or 877-927-8387
Jackson Vet Center	1755 Lelia Dr. Suite 104 Jackson, MS 39216	MS	601-965-5727 Or 877-927-8387
Billings Vet Center	2795 Enterprise Ave., Suite 1 Billings, MT 59102	MT	406-657-6071 Or 406-657-6071
Great Falls Vet Center	615 2nd Avenue North Great Falls, MT 59401	MT	406-452-9048 Or 877-927-8387
Kalispell Vet Center	690 North Meridian Road, Suite 101 Kalispell, MT 59901	MT	406-257-7308 Or 877-927-8387
Missoula Vet Center	500 N. Higgins Avenue, Suite 202 Missoula, MT 59802	MT	406-721-4918
Charlotte Vet Center	2114 Ben Craig Dr., Suite 300 Charlotte, NC 28262	NC	704-549-8025 Or 877-927-8387
Fayetteville Vet Center	4140 Ramsey St. Suite 110 Fayetteville, NC 28311	NC	910-488-6252 Or 877-927-8387
Greensboro Vet Center	3515 W Market St., Suite 120 Greensboro, NC 27406	NC	336-333-5366 Or 877-927-8387
Greenville, NC Vet Center	1021 W.H. Smith Blvd., Suite A 100 Greenville, NC 27834	NC	252-355-7920 Or 877-927-8387
Jacksonville Vet Center	110A Branchwood Dr Jacksonville, NC 28546	NC	910-577-1100 Or 910-577-1100
Raleigh Vet Center	1649 Old Louisburg Rd. Raleigh, NC 27604	NC	919-856-4616 Or 877-927-8387

Bismarck Vet Center	619 Riverwood Drive, Suite 105 Bismarck, ND 58504	ND	701-224-9751 Or 701-224-9751
Fargo Vet Center	3310 Fiechtner Drive. Suite 100 Fargo, ND 58103-8730	ND	701-237-0942
Minot Vet Center	1400 20th Avenue SW Ste 2 Minot, ND 58701	ND	701-852-0177 Or 877-927-8387
Lincoln Vet Center	3119 O Street, Suite A Lincoln, NE 68510	NE	402-476-9736 Or 877-927-8387
Omaha Vet Center	3047 S 72nd Street Omaha, NE 68124	NE	402-346-6735 Or 877-927-8387
1A RCS Northeast Regional Office	15 Dartmouth Drive, Suite 202 Auburn, NH 03032	NH	603-623-4204 Or 877-927-8387
Berlin Vet Center	515 Main Street Suite 2 Gorham, NH 03581	NH	603-752-2571 Or 877-927-8387
Keene Vet Center Outstation	640 Marlboro Rd. (Route 101) Keene, NH 03431	NH	603-358-4950 Or 603-358-4951
Manchester Vet Center	1461 Hooksett Rd., B6 Hooksett, NH 03106	NH	603-668-7060 Or 603-668-7060
Bloomfield Vet Center	2 Broad St. Suite 703 Bloomfield, NJ 07003	NJ	973-748-0980 Or 877-927-8387
Lakewood Vet Center	1255 Route 70; Unit 22N, Parkway Seventy Plaza Lakewood, NJ 08701	NJ	908-607-6364
Secaucus Vet Center	110A Meadowlands Parkway, Suite 102 Secaucus, NJ 07094	NJ	201-223-7787 Or 877-927-8387
Trenton Vet Center	934 Parkway Ave. Suite 201 Ewing, NJ 08618	NJ	609-882-5744 Or 877-927-8387
Ventnor Vet Center	6601 Ventnor Ave. Suite 105, Ventnor Bldg. Ventnor, NJ 08406	NJ	609-487-8387 Or 877-927-8387
Albuquerque Vet Center	1600 Mountain Road NW Albuquerque, NM 87104	NM	505-346-6562 Or 877-927-8387
Farmington Vet Center	4251 E. Main Suite A Farmington, NM 87402	NM	505-327-9684 Or 877-927-8387
Las Cruces Vet Center	230 S. Water Street Las Cruces, NM 88001	NM	575-523-9826 Or 877-927-8387
Santa Fe Vet Center	2209 Brothers Road Suite 110 Santa Fe, NM 87505	NM	505-988-6562 Or 877-927-8387
Henderson Vet Center	400 North Stephanie, Suite 180 Henderson, NV 89014	NV	702-791-9100 Or 877-927-8387
Las Vegas Vet Center	1919 S. Jones Blvd., Suite A Las Vegas, NV 89146	NV	702-251-7873 Or 877-927-8387
Reno Vet Center	5580 Mill St. Suite 600 Reno, NV 89502	NV	775-323-1294 Or 877-927-8387
Albany Vet Center	17 Computer Drive West Albany, NY 12205	NY	518-626-5130 Or 877-927-8387
Babylon Vet Center	116 West Main St. Babylon, NY 11702	NY	631-661-3930 Or 631-661-3930

Binghamton Vet Center	53 Chenango Street Binghamton, NY 13901	NY	607-722-2393 Or 877-927-8387
Bronx Vet Center	2471 Morris Ave., Suite 1A Bronx, NY 10468	NY	718-367-3500 Or 877-927-8387
Brooklyn Vet Center	25 Chapel St. Suite 604 Brooklyn, NY 11201	NY	718-630-2830 Or 877-927-8387
Buffalo Vet Center	2372 Sweet Home Road, Suite 1 Buffalo, NY 14228	NY	716-862-7350 Or 877-927-8387
Harlem Vet Center	2279 - 3rd Avenue, 2nd Floor New York, NY 10035	NY	646-273-8139 Or 877-927-8387
Manhattan Vet Center	32 Broadway 2nd Floor - Suite 200 New York, NY 10004	NY	212-742-9591 Or 877-927-8387
Middletown Vet Center	726 East Main Street, Suite 203 Middletown, NY 10940	NY	845-342-9917 Or 877-927-8387
Nassau Vet Center	970 South Broadway Hicksville, NY 11801	NY	516-348-0088 Or 877-927-8387
Queens Vet Center	75-10B 91 Ave. Woodhaven, NY 11421	NY	718-296-2871 Or 877-927-8387
Rochester Vet Center	2000 S. Winton Road, Bldg 5, Ste. 201 Rochester, NY 14618	NY	585-232-5040 Or 877-927-8387
Staten Island Vet Center	60 Bay Street Staten Island, NY 10301	NY	718-816-4499 Or 877-927-8387
Syracuse Vet Center	109 Pine Street, Suite 101 Syracuse, NY 13210	NY	315-478-7127 Or 315-478-7127
Watertown Vet Center	210 Court Street, Suie 20 Watertown, NY 13601	NY	315-782-5479 Or 877-927-8387
White Plains Vet Center	300 Hamilton Ave. Suite C White Plains, NY 10601	NY	914-682-6250 Or 877-927-8387
Cincinnati Vet Center	801B W. 8th St. Suite 126 Cincinnati, OH 45203	OH	513-763-3500 Or 877-927-8387
Cleveland Maple Heights Vet Center	5310 1/2 Warrensville Center Rd Maple Heights, OH 44137	OH	216-707-7901 Or 216-707-7901
Columbus Vet Center	30 Spruce Street Columbus, OH 43215	OH	614-257-5550 Or 877-927-8387
Dayton Vet Center	627 Edwin C. Moses Blvd.,6th Floor, East Medical Plaza Dayton, OH 45417	OH	937-461-9150 Or 877-927-8387
McCafferty Vet Center Outstation	4242 Lorain Avenue Suite 203 Cleveland, OH 44113	OH	216-939-0784 Or 877-927-8387
Parma Vet Center	5700 Pearl Road Suite 102 Parma, OH 44129	OH	440-845-5023 Or 877-927-8387
Stark County Vet Center	601 Cleveland Ave N, Suite C Canton, OH 44702	OH	330-454-3120 Or 877-927-8387
Toledo Vet Center	1565 S. Byrne Road, Suite 104 Toledo, OH 43614	OH	419-213-7533 Or 877-927-8387
Lawton Vet Center	1016 SW C Avenue, Suite B Lawton, OK 73501	OK	580-585-5880 Or 877-927-8387

Oklahoma City Vet Center	1024 NW 47th St. Suite B Oklahoma City, OK 73118	OK	405-456-5184 Or 877-927-8387
Tulsa Vet Center	14002 E. 21st Street, Suite # 200 Tulsa, OK 74134-1412	OK	918-628-2760 Or 877-927-8387
Central Oregon Vet Center	1645 NE Forbes Rd. Suite 105 Bend, OR 97701	OR	541-749-2112 Or 877-927-8387
Eugene Vet Center	190 East 11th Avenue, Suite 200 Eugene, OR 97401	OR	541-465-6918 Or 877-927-8387
Grants Pass Vet Center	211 S.E. 10th St. Grants Pass, OR 97526	OR	541-479-6912 Or 877-927-8387
Portland Vet Center	1505 NE 122nd Ave, Suite 110 Portland, OR 97230	OR	503-688-5361 Or 877-927-8387
Salem Vet Center	2645 Portland Road, Suite 250 Salem, OR 97301	OR	503-362-9911
Bucks County Vet Center	2 Canal's End Plaza, Suite 201B Bristol, PA 19007	PA	215-823-4590 Or 877-927-8387
DuBois Vet Center	100 Meadow Lane, Suite 8 DuBois, PA 15801	PA	814-372-2095 Or 877-927-8387
Erie Vet Center	240 W. 11th St., Erie Metro Center, Suite 105 Erie, PA 16501	PA	814-453-7955 Or 877-927-8387
Harrisburg Vet Center	1500 N. Second Street Suite 2 Harrisburg, PA 17102	PA	717-782-3954 Or 877-927-8387
Lancaster Vet Center	1817 Olde Homestead Lane, Suite 207 Lancaster, PA 17601	PA	717-283-0735 Or 877-927-8387
McKeesport Vet Center	2001 Lincoln Way McKeesport, PA 15131	PA	412-678-7704 Or 412-678-7704
Montgomery County Vet Center	320 E. Johnson Hwy, Suite 201 Norristown, PA 19401	PA	215-823-5245 Or 877-927-8387
Philadelphia Vet Center	801 Arch Street Suite 502 Philadelphia, PA 19107	PA	215-627-0238 Or 877-927-8387
Philadelphia Vet Center NE	101 E. Olney Avenue Suite C-7 Philadelphia, PA 19120	PA	215-924-4670 Or 877-927-8387
Pittsburgh Vet Center	2500 Baldwick Rd, Suite 15 Pittsburgh, PA 15205	PA	412-920-1765
Scranton Vet Center	1002 Pittston Ave. Scranton, PA 18505	PA	570-344-2676 Or 877-927-8387
Williamsport Vet Center	49 E. Fourth Street Suite 104 Williamsport, PA 17701	PA	570-327-5281 Or 877-927-8387
Arecibo Vet Center	50 Gonzalo Marin St Arecibo, PR 00612	PR	787-879-4510 Or 877-927-8387
Ponce Vet Center	35 Mayor Street, Suite 1 Ponce, PR 00730	PR	787-841-3260 Or 877-927-8387
San Juan Vet Center	Cond. Medical Center Plaza Suite LC 8, 9 & 11, Urb. La Riviera Rio Piedras, PR 0921	PR	787-749-4409 Or 877-927-8387
Providence Vet Center	2038 Warwick Ave Warwick, RI 02889	RI	401-739-0167 Or 877-927-8387
Charleston Vet Center	5603-A Rivers Ave. N. Charleston, SC 29406	SC	843-789-7000 Or 877-927-8387

Columbia Vet Center	1710 Richland Street, Suite A Columbia, SC 29201	SC	803-765-9944 Or 877-927-8387
Greenville, SC Vet Center	3 Caledon Court, Suite B Greenville, SC 29615	SC	864-271-2711 Or 877-927-8387
Horry County Vet Center	2024 Corporate Centre Dr, Suite 103 Myrtle Beach, SC 29577	SC	843-232-2441 Or 877-927-8381
Horry County Vet Center	2024 Corporate Centre Dr, Suite 103 Myrtle Beach, SC 29577	SC	843-465-0713 Or 877-927-8387
Pine Ridge Vet Center Outstation	P.O. Box 910 105 E. Hwy 18 Martin, SD 57747	SD	605-685-1300 Or 877-927-8387
Rapid City Vet Center	621 6th St, Suite 101 Rapid City, SD 57701	SD	605-348-0077 Or 877-927-8387
Sioux Falls Vet Center	3200 W 49th Street Sioux Falls, SD 57106	SD	605-330-4552 Or 877-927-8387
Chattanooga Vet Center	951 Eastgate Loop Road Bldg. 5700 - Suite 300 Chattanooga, TN 37411	TN	423-855-6570 Or 877-927-8387
Johnson City Vet Center	2203 McKinley Road, Suite 254 Johnson City, TN 37604	TN	423-928-8387 Or 877-927-8387
Knoxville Vet Center	2817 E. Magnolia Ave Knoxville, TN 37914	TN	865-633-0000 Or 877-927-8387
Memphis Vet Center	1407 Union Ave., Suite 410 Memphis, TN 38104	TN	901-544-0173 Or 877-927-8387
Nashville Vet Center	1420 Donelson Pike Suite A-5 Nashville, TN 37217	TN	615-366-1220 Or 877-927-8387
3B RCS South Central Regional Office	4500 S. Lancaster Rd. Building 69 Dallas, TX 75216	TX	214-857-1254 Or 877-927-8387
Amarillo Vet Center	3414 Olsen Blvd. Suite E Amarillo, TX 79109	TX	806-354-9779 Or 877-927-8387
Austin Vet Center	2015 S. I.H. 35, Southcliff Bldg., Suite 101 Austin, TX 78741	TX	512-416-1314 Or 877-927-8387
Corpus Christi Vet Center	4646 Corona Suite 250 Corpus Christi, TX 78411	TX	361-854-9961 Or 877-927-8387
Dallas County Vet Center	502 West Kearney, Suite 300 Mesquite, TX 75149	TX	972-288-8030 Or 877-927-8387
Dallas Vet Center	10501 N. Central Expy Suite 213 Dallas, TX 75231	TX	214-361-5896 Or 877-927-8387
El Paso Vet Center	1155 Westmoreland Suite 121 El Paso, TX 79925	TX	915-772-0013 Or 877-927-8387
Fort Worth Vet Center	1305 W. Magnolia St. Suite B Ft. Worth, TX 76104	TX	817-921-9095 Or 877-927-8387
Harris County Vet Center	14300 Cornerstone Village Dr., Suite 110 Houston, TX 77014	TX	281-537-7812
Houston Vet Center	3000 Richmond Avenue, Suite 355 Houston, TX 77098	TX	713-523-0884 Or 713-523-0884
Houston West Vet Center	701 N. Post Oak Road Suite 102 Houston, TX 77024	TX	713-682-2288 Or 877-927-8387
Jefferson County Vet Center	990 IH10 North, Suite 180 Beaumont, TX 77702	TX	409-347-0124

Killeen Heights Vet Center	302 Millers Crossing, Suite #4 Harker Heights, TX 76548	TX	254-953-7100 Or 877-927-8387
Laredo Vet Center	6999 McPherson Road Suite 102 Laredo, TX 78041	TX	956-723-4680 Or 877-927-8387
Lubbock Vet Center	3106 50th st suite 400 Lubbock, TX 79413	TX	806-792-9782 Or 877-927-8387
McAllen Vet Center	2108 S M Street, MedPoint IV, Unit 2 McAllen, TX 78503	TX	956-631-2147 Or 877-927-8387
Midland Vet Center	4400 N. Midland Drive, Suite 540 Midland, TX 79707	TX	432-697-8222 Or 432-697-8222
San Antonio NE Vet Center	9504 IH 35 N, Suite 214 & 219 San Antonio, TX 78233	TX	210-650-0422 Or 877-927-8387
San Antonio NW Vet Center	9910 W Loop 1604 N, Suite 126 San Antonio, TX 78254	TX	210-688-0606 Or 877-927-8387
Tarrant County Vet Center	3337 W. Pioneer Pkwy, Northlake Center Pantego, TX 76013	TX	817-274-0981 Or 877-927-8387
Taylor County Vet Center	3564 N 6th Street Abilene, TX 79603	TX	325-232-7925 Or 877-927-8387
Provo Vet Center	1807 No. 1120 West Provo, UT 84604	UT	801-377-1117 Or 877-927-8387
Salt Lake Vet Center	22 West Fireclay Avenue Murray, UT 84107	UT	801-266-1499 Or 877-927-8387
St. George Vet Center	1664 South Dixie Drive, Suite C-102 St. George, UT 84770-4494	UT	435-673-4494 Or 877-927-8387
Alexandria Vet Center	6940 South Kings Highway #204 Alexandria, VA 22310	VA	703-360-8633 Or 877-927-8387
Norfolk Vet Center	1711 Church Street, Suites A&B Norfolk, VA 23504	VA	757-623-7584 Or 877-927-8387
Richmond Vet Center	4902 Fitzhugh Avenue Richmond, VA 23230	VA	804-353-8958 Or 877-927-8387
Roanoke Vet Center	350 Albemarle Ave., SW Roanoke, VA 24016	VA	540-342-9726 Or 877-927-8387
Virginia Beach County Vet Center	324 Southport Circle, Suite 102 Virginia Beach, VA 23452	VA	757-248-3665 Or 877-927-8387
St. Croix Vet Center Outstation	The Village Mall, RR 2 Box 10553 Kingshill St. Croix, VI 00850	VI	340-778-5553 Or 877-927-8387
St. Thomas Vet Center Outstation	50 Estate Thomas,Medical Foundation Buiding Suite 101 St. Thomas, VI 00802	VI	340-774-5017 Or 877-927-8387
South Burlington Vet Center	359 Dorset St. South Burlington, VT 05403	VT	802-862-1806 Or 877-927-8387
White River Junction Vet Center	222 Holiday Drive, GIlman Office, Bldg. 2 White River Junction, VT 05001	VT	802-295-2908 Or 877-927-8387
Bellingham Vet Center	3800 Byron Ave Suite 124 Bellingham, WA 98229	WA	360-733-9226 Or 877-927-8387
Everett Vet Center	3311 Wetmore Avenue Everett, WA 98201	WA	425-252-9701 Or 425-252-9701

Federal Way Vet Center	32020 32nd Ave South Suite 110 Federal Way, WA 98001	WA	253-838-3090 Or 877-927-8387
Seattle Vet Center	4735 E Marginal Way S, Room 2401 Seattle, WA 98134	WA	206-553-2706 Or 877-927-8387
Spokane Vet Center	13109 E Mirabeau Parkway Spokane, WA 99216	WA	509-444-8387 Or 877-927-8387
Tacoma Vet Center	4916 Center St. Suite E Tacoma, WA 98409	WA	253-565-7038 Or 877-927-8387
Walla Walla County Vet Center	1104 West Poplar Walla Walla, WA 99362	WA	509-526-8387 Or 877-927-8387
Yakima Vet Center	2119 W. Lincoln Ave Yakima, WA 98902	WA	509-457-2736 Or 509-457-2736
Green Bay Vet Center	1600 S. Ashland Ave Green Bay, WI 54304	WI	920-435-5650 Or 877-927-8387
La Crosse Vet Center	20 Copeland Ave. La Crosse, WI 54603	WI	608-782-4403 Or 877-927-8387
Madison Vet Center	706 Williamson Street Madison, WI 53703	WI	608-264-5342 Or 877-927-8387
Milwaukee Vet Center	7910 N. 76th Street, Suite 100 Milwaukee, WI 53223	WI	414-434-1311 Or 414-434-1311
Wausau Vet Center	605 S 24th Ave, Suite 24 Wausau, WI 54401	WI	715-842-1724 Or 715-842-1724
Beckley Vet Center	1000 Johnstown Road Beckley, WV 25801	WV	304-252-8220 Or 877-927-8387
Charleston Vet Center	521 Central Avenue Charleston, WV 25302	WV	304-343-3825 Or 877-927-8387
Huntington Vet Center	3135 16th Street Road Suite 11 Huntington, WV 25701	WV	304-523-8387 Or 877-927-8387
Logan Vet Center Outstation	21 Veterans Avenue Henlawson, WV 25624	WV	304-752-4453 Or 877-927-8387
Martinsburg Vet Center	300 Foxcroft Ave. Suite 100 Martinburg, WV 25401	WV	304-263-6776 Or 877-927-8387
Morgantown Vet Center	34 Commerce Drive, Suite 101 Morgantown, WV 26501	WV	304-291-4303 Or 877-927-8387
Parkersburg Vet Center Outstation	2311 Ohio Avenue, Suite D Pakersburg, WV 26101	WV	304-485-1599 Or 877-927-8387
Princeton Vet Center	905 Mercer Street Princeton, WV 24740	WV	304-425-5653 Or 877-927-8387
Wheeling Vet Center	1058 Bethlehem Blvd. Wheeling, WV 26003	WV	304-232-0587 Or 304-232-0587
Casper Vet Center	1030 North Poplar Casper, WY 82601	WY	307-261-5355
Cheyenne Vet Center	3219 E Pershing Blvd Cheyenne, WY 82001	WY	307-778-7370 Or 877-927-8387

PTSD Treatment Facilities by State

Facility	Address	State	Phone
Alaska VA Healthcare System	1201 North Muldoon Road Anchorage, AK 99504	AK	907-257-4700 Or 907-257-4700
Birmingham VA Medical Center	700 S. 19th Street Birmingham, AL 35233	AL	205-933-8101
Central Alabama Veterans Health Care System East Campus	2400 Hospital Road Tuskegee, AL 36083-5001	AL	334-727-0550 Or 334-727-0550
Central Alabama Veterans Health Care System West Campus	215 Perry Hill Road Montgomery, AL 36109-3798	AL	334-272-4670 Or 800-214-8387
Tuscaloosa VA Medical Center	3701 Loop Road, East Tuscaloosa, AL 35404	AL	205-554-2000 Or 205-554-2000
Central Arkansas Veterans Healthcare System Eugene J. Towbin Healthcare Center	2200 Fort Roots Drive North Little Rock, AR 72114-1706	AR	501-257-1000
Central Arkansas Veterans Healthcare System John L. McClellan Memorial Veterans Hospital	4300 West 7th Street Little Rock, AR 72205-5484	AR	501-257-1000
Veterans Health Care System of the Ozarks	1100 N. College Avenue Fayetteville, AR 72703	AR	479-443-4301 Or 800-691-8387
Northern Arizona VA Health Care System	500 North Highway 89 Prescott, AZ 86313	AZ	928-445-4860 Or 928-445-4860
Phoenix VA Health Care System	650 E. Indian School Road Phoenix, AZ 85012	AZ	602-277-5551 Or 800-554-7174
Southern Arizona VA Health Care System	3601 South 6th Avenue Tucson, AZ 85723	AZ	520-792-1450 Or 800-470-8262
Livermore	4951 Arroyo Road Livermore, CA 94550	CA	925-373-4700
Menlo Park	795 Willow Road Menlo Park, CA 94025	CA	650-614-9997
San Francisco VA Medical Center	4150 Clement Street San Francisco, CA 94121	CA	415-221-4810 Or 877-487-2838
VA Central California Health Care System	2615 E. Clinton Avenue Fresno, CA 93703	CA	559-225-6100 Or 559-225-6100
VA Greater Los Angeles Healthcare System (GLA)	11301 Wilshire Boulevard Los Angeles, CA 90073	CA	310-478-3711
VA Loma Linda Healthcare System	11201 Benton Street Loma Linda, CA 92357	CA	909-825-7084 Or 909-825-7084
VA Long Beach Healthcare System	5901 E. 7th Street Long Beach, CA 90822	CA	562-826-8000 Or 562-826-8000
VA Northern California Health Care System	10535 Hospital Way Mather, CA 95655	CA	800-382-8387 Or 800-382-8387
VA Palo Alto Health Care System	3801 Miranda Avenue Palo Alto, CA 94304-1290	CA	650-493-5000
VA San Diego Healthcare System	3350 La Jolla Village Drive San Diego, CA 92161	CA	858-552-8585

Grand Junction VA Medical Center	2121 North Avenue Grand Junction, CO 81501	CO	970-242-0731 Or 970-242-0731
VA Eastern Colorado Health Care System(ECHCS)	1055 Clermont Street Denver, CO 80220	CO	303-399-8020
VA Connecticut Healthcare System	950 Campbell Avenue West Haven, CT 06516	CT	203-932-5711
VA Connecticut Healthcare System, Newington Campus	555 Willard Avenue Newington, CT 06111	CT	860-666-6951
VA Connecticut Healthcare System, West Haven Campus	950 Campbell Avenue West Haven, CT 06516	CT	203-932-5711
Washington DC VA Medical Center	50 Irving Street, NW Washington, DC 20422	DC	202-745-8000 Or 202-745-8000
Wilmington VA Medical Center	1601 Kirkwood Highway Wilmington, DE 19805	DE	302-994-2511 Or 800-461-8262
C.W. Bill Young VA Medical Center	10000 Bay Pines Blvd Bay Pines, FL 33744 Mailing Address: P.O.Box 5005 Bay Pines, FL 33744	FL	727-398-6661 Or 727-398-6661
James A. Haley Veterans' Hospital	13000 Bruce B. Downs Blvd. Tampa, FL 33612	FL	813-972-2000 Or 813-972-2000
Lake City VAMC, NF/SGVHS	619 S. Marion Avenue Lake City, FL 32025-5808	FL	386-755-3016 Or 800-308-8387
Lakemont Campus	2500 S. Lakemont Ave Orlando, FL 32814	FL	407-629-1599
Malcom Randall VAMC, NF/SGVHS	1601 S.W. Archer Road Gainesville, FL 32608-1197	FL	352-376-1611 Or 800-324-8387
Miami VA Healthcare System	1201 N.W. 16th Street Miami, FL 33125	FL	305-575-7000 Or 888-276-1785
North Florida/South Georgia Veterans Health System	1601 S.W. Archer Road Gainesville, FL 32608	FL	352-376-1611
Orlando VA Medical Center	5201 Raymond Street, Orlando, FL 32803	FL	407-629-1599 Or 407-629-1599
West Palm Beach VAMC	7305 N. Military Trail West Palm Beach, FL 33410-6400	FL	561-422-8262 Or 561-422-8262
Atlanta VA Medical Center	1670 Clairmont Road Decatur, GA 30033	GA	404-321-6111
Carl Vinson VA Medical Center	1826 Veterans Blvd. Dublin, GA 31021	GA	478-272-1210
Charlie Norwood VA Medical Center	1 Freedom Way Augusta, GA 30904-6285	GA	706-733-0188 Or 706-733-0188
VA Pacific Islands Health Care System	459 Patterson Road Honolulu, HI 96819-1522	HI	808-433-0600 Or 808-433-0600
Iowa City VA Health Care System	601 Highway 6 West Iowa City, IA 52246-2208	IA	319-338-0581 Or 319-338-0581
VA Central Iowa Health Care System	3600 30th Street Des Moines, IA 50310-5774	IA	515-699-5999 Or 515-699-5999
Boise VA Medical Center	500 West Fort Street Boise, ID 83702	ID	208-422-1000
Captain James A. Lovell Federal Health Care Center	3001 Green Bay Road North Chicago, IL 60064	IL	847-688-1900 Or 800-393-0865
Edward Hines Jr. VA Hospital	5000 South 5th Avenue Hines, IL 60141	IL	708-202-8387

Jesse Brown VA Medical Center	820 South Damen Avenue Chicago, IL 60612	IL	312-569-8387 Or 312-569-8387
Marion VA Medical Center	2401 West Main Street Marion, IL 62959	IL	618-997-5311 Or 618-997-5311
VA Illiana Health Care System	1900 East Main Street Danville, IL 61832-5198	IL	217-554-3000 Or 217-554-3000
Richard L. Roudebush VA Medical Center (Indianapolis VA Medical Center)	1481 W. 10th Street Indianapolis, IN 46202	IN	317-554-0000 Or 317-554-0000
VA Northern Indiana Health Care System	2121 Lake Ave. Fort Wayne, IN 46805	IN	260-426-5431 Or 206-426-5431
VA Northern Indiana Health Care System - Marion Campus	1700 East 38th Street Marion, IN 46953-4589	IN	765-674-3321 Or 800-360-8387
VA Northern Indiana Health Care System-Fort Wayne Campus	2121 Lake Ave. Fort Wayne, IN 46805	IN	260-426-5431 Or 800-360-8387
Robert J. Dole VA Medical Center	5500 E. Kellogg Wichita, KS 67218	KS	316-685-2221 Or 316-685-2221
VA Eastern Kansas Health Care System - Colmery-O'Neil VA Medical Center	2200 SW Gage Boulevard Topeka, KS 66622	KS	785-350-3111 Or 785-350-3111
VA Eastern Kansas Health Care System - Dwight D. Eisenhower VA Medical Center	4101 S. 4th Street Leavenworth, KS 66048-5055	KS	913-682-2000 Or 913-682-2000
Lexington VA Medical Center	1101 Veterans Drive Lexington, KY 40502-2236	KY	859-233-4511
Lexington VAMC: Cooper Division	1101 Veterans Drive Lexington, KY 40502-2236	KY	859-281-4900 Or 859-233-4511
Lexington VAMC: Leestown Division	2250 Leestown Rd Lexington, KY 40511-1052	KY	859-233-4511 Or 859-281-4900
Robley Rex VA Medical Center	800 Zorn Avenue Louisville, KY 40206	KY	502-287-4000 Or 800-376-8387
Alexandria VA Health Care System	(mail: Department of Veteran Affairs Medical Center, P.O. Box 69004 Alexandria, LA 71306-9004	LA	318-473-0010 Or 800-375-8387
Overton Brooks VA Medical Center	510 E. Stoner Ave. Shreveport, LA 71101-4295	LA	318-221-8411 Or 318-221-8411
Southeast Louisiana Veterans Health Care System	1601 Perdido Street New Orleans, LA 70112	LA	800-935-8387 Or 504-412-3700
Edith Nourse Rogers Memorial Veterans Hospital	200 Springs Rd. Bedford, MA 01730	MA	781-687-2000 Or 800-838-6331
VA Boston Healthcare System	150 South Huntington Avenue Jamaica Plain, MA 02130	MA	617-232-9500
VA Boston Healthcare System, Brockton Campus	940 Belmont Street Brockton, MA 02301	MA	508-583-4500 Or 508-583-4500
VA Boston Healthcare System, Jamaica Plain Campus	150 South Huntington Avenue Jamaica Plain, MA 02130	MA	617-232-9500 Or 617-232-9500
VA Boston Healthcare System, West Roxbury Campus	1400 VFW Parkway West Roxbury, MA 02132	MA	617-323-7700 Or 617-323-7700
VA Central Western Massachusetts Healthcare System	421 North Main Street Leeds, MA 01053-9764	MA	413-584-4040

Baltimore VA Medical Center - VA Maryland Health Care System	10 North Greene Street Baltimore, MD 21201	MD	410-605-7000 Or 410-605-7000
Loch Raven VA Community Living & Rehabilitation Center	3900 Loch Raven Boulevard Baltimore, MD 21218	MD	410-605-7000 Or 410-605-7000
Perry Point VA Medical Center - VA Maryland Health Care System	VA Medical Center Perry Point, MD 21902	MD	410-642-2411 Or 410-642-2411
VA Maryland Health Care System	10 North Greene Street Baltimore, MD 21201	MD	410-605-7000
VA Maine Healthcare System - Togus	1 VA Center Augusta, ME 04330	ME	207-623-8411 Or 207-623-8411
Aleda E. Lutz VA Medical Center	1500 Weiss Street Saginaw, MI 48602	MI	989-497-2500 Or 989-497-2500
Battle Creek VA Medical Center	5500 Armstrong Road Battle Creek, MI 49037	MI	269-966-5600 Or 269-966-5600
John D. Dingell VA Medical Center	4646 John R Detroit, MI 48201	MI	313-576-1000 Or 800-511-8056
Oscar G. Johnson VA Medical Center	325 East H Street Iron Mountain, MI 49801	MI	906-774-3300
VA Ann Arbor Healthcare System	2215 Fuller Road Ann Arbor, MI 48105	MI	734-769-7100 Or 734-769-7100
Minneapolis VA Health Care System	One Veterans Drive Minneapolis, MN 55417	MN	612-725-2000 Or 612-725-2000
St. Cloud VA Health Care System	4801 Veterans Drive St. Cloud, MN 56303	MN	320-252-1670 Or 320-252-1670
Harry S. Truman Memorial	800 Hospital Drive Columbia, MO 65201-5297	MO	573-814-6000 Or 573-814-6000
John J. Pershing VA Medical Center	1500 N. Westwood Blvd. Poplar Bluff, MO 63901	MO	573-686-4151 Or 573-686-4151
Kansas City VA Medical Center	4801 Linwood Boulevard Kansas City, MO 64128	MO	816-861-4700
VA St. Louis Health Care System	1 Jefferson Barracks Drive Saint Louis, MO 63125	MO	314-652-4100
VA St. Louis Health Care System - Jefferson Barracks Division	1 Jefferson Barracks Drive Saint Louis, MO 63125	MO	314-652-4100
VA St. Louis Health Care System - John Cochran Division	915 North Grand Blvd. Saint Louis, MO 63106	MO	314-652-4100
G.V. (Sonny) Montgomery VA Medical Center	1500 E. Woodrow Wilson Drive Jackson, MS 39216	MS	601-362-4471
Gulf Coast Veterans Health Care System	400 Veterans Avenue Biloxi, MS 39531	MS	228-523-5000
VA Montana Health Care System	3687 Veterans Drive, P.O.BOX 1500 Fort Harrison, MT 59636	MT	406-442-6410
Asheville VA Medical Center	1100 Tunnel Road Asheville, NC 28805	NC	828-298-7911
Durham VA Medical Center	508 Fulton Street Durham, NC 27705	NC	919-286-0411 Or 888-878-6890
Fayetteville VA Medical Center	2300 Ramsey Street Fayetteville, NC 28301	NC	910-488-2120 Or 910-488-2120
Salisbury - W.G. (Bill) Hefner VA Medical Center	1601 Brenner Avenue Salisbury, NC 28144	NC	704-638-9000 Or 704-638-9000
Fargo VA Healthcare System	2101 Elm Street N. Fargo, ND 58102	ND	701-232-3241 Or 701-232-3241

Omaha - VA Nebraska-Western Iowa Health Care System	4101 Woolworth Avenue Omaha, NE 68105	NE	402-346-8800 Or 402-346-8800
Manchester VA Medical Center	718 Smyth Road Manchester, NH 03104	NH	603-624-4366 Or 800-892-8384
East Orange Campus of the VA New Jersey Health Care System	385 Tremont Avenue East Orange, NJ 07018	NJ	973-676-1000
Lyons Campus of the VA New Jersey Health Care System	151 Knollcroft Road Lyons, NJ 07939	NJ	908-647-0180
VA New Jersey Health Care System	385 Tremont Avenue East Orange, NJ 07018	NJ	973-676-1000
New Mexico VA Health Care System	1501 San Pedro Drive, SE Albuquerque, NM 87108-5153	NM	505-265-1711 Or 505-265-1711
VA Sierra Nevada Health Care System	975 Kirman Avenue Reno, NV 89502	NV	775-786-7200 Or 775-786-7200
VA Southern Nevada Healthcare System (VASNHS)	6900 North Pecos Road North Las Vegas, NV 89086	NV	702-791-9000
Albany VA Medical Center: Samuel S. Stratton	113 Holland Avenue Albany, NY 12208	NY	518-626-5000 Or 518-626-5000
Bath VA Medical Center	76 Veterans Avenue Bath, NY 14810	NY	607-664-4000 Or 607-664-4000
Brooklyn Campus of the VA NY Harbor Healthcare System	800 Poly Place Brooklyn, NY 11209	NY	718-836-6600
Canandaigua VA Medical Center	400 Fort Hill Avenue Canandaigua, NY 14424	NY	585-394-2000 Or 585-394-2000
Castle Point Campus of the VA Hudson Valley Health Care System	41 Castle Point Road Wappingers Falls, NY 12590	NY	845-831-2000
Franklin Delano Roosevelt Campus of the VA Hudson Valley Health Care System (Montrose)	2094 Albany Post Rd. Montrose, NY 10548	NY	914-737-4400
James J. Peters VA Medical Center (Bronx, NY)	130 West Kingsbridge Road Bronx, NY 10468	NY	718-584-9000
Manhattan Campus of the VA NY Harbor Healthcare System	423 East 23rd Street New York, NY 10010	NY	212-686-7500
Northport VA Medical Center	79 Middleville Road Northport, NY 11768	NY	631-261-4400 Or 631-261-4400
Syracuse VA Medical Center	800 Irving Avenue Syracuse, NY 13210	NY	315-425-4400 Or 315-425-4400
VA Hudson Valley Health Care System	2094 Albany Post Rd. Montrose, NY 10548	NY	914-737-4400
VA NY Harbor Healthcare System	423 East 23rd Street New York, NY 10010	NY	
VA Western New York Healthcare System	3495 Bailey Avenue Buffalo, NY 14215	NY	716-834-9200 Or 716-834-9200
VA Western New York Healthcare System at Batavia	222 Richmond Avenue Batavia, NY 14020	NY	585-297-1000
VA Western New York Healthcare System at Buffalo	3495 Bailey Avenue Buffalo, NY 14215	NY	716-834-9200 Or 716-834-9200
Chalmers P. Wylie Ambulatory Care Center	420 N James Road Columbus, OH 43219	OH	614-257-5200
Chillicothe VA Medical Center	17273 State Route 104 Chillicothe, OH 45601	OH	740-773-1141
Cincinnati VA Medical Center	3200 Vine Street Cincinnati, OH 45220	OH	513-861-3100

Dayton VA Medical Center	4100 W. 3rd Street Dayton, OH 45428	OH	937-268-6511 Or 937-268-6511
Louis Stokes Cleveland VA Medical Center	10701 East Boulevard Cleveland, OH 44106	OH	216-791-3800
Jack C. Montgomery VAMC	1011 Honor Heights Drive Muskogee, OK 74401	OK	918-577-3000 Or 918-577-3000
Oklahoma City VA Medical Center	921 N.E. 13th Street Oklahoma City, OK 73104	OK	405-456-1000 Or 405-456-1000
Portland VA Medical Center	3710 SW U.S. Veterans Hospital Road Portland, OR 97239	OR	503-220-8262 Or 503-220-8262
VA Roseburg Healthcare System	913 NW Garden Valley Blvd. Roseburg, OR 97471-6513	OR	541-440-1000 Or 800-549-8387
White City or VA Southern Oregon Rehabilitation Center	8495 Crater Lake Hwy. White City, OR 97503	OR	541-826-2111
Altoona - James E. Van Zandt VA Medical Center	2907 Pleasant Valley Boulevard Altoona, PA 16602-4377	PA	814-943-8164 Or 814-943-8164
Coatesville VA Medical Center	1400 Black Horse Hill Road Coatesville, PA 19320-2096	PA	610-384-7711 Or 610-384-7711
Erie VA Medical Center	135 East 38th Street Erie, PA 16504	PA	800-274-8387 Or 814-868-8661
Lebanon VA Medical Center	1700 South Lincoln Avenue Lebanon, PA 17042	PA	717-272-6621 Or 800-409-8771
Philadelphia VA Medical Center	3900 Woodland Avenue Philadelphia, PA 19104	PA	215-823-5800 Or 215-823-5800
VA Butler Healthcare	325 New Castle Road Butler, PA 16001-2480	PA	800-362-8262
VA Pittsburgh Healthcare System	University Drive Pittsburgh, PA 15240	PA	412-360-6000
VA Pittsburgh Healthcare System, H.J. Heinz Campus	1010 Delafield Road Pittsburgh, PA 15215	PA	412-360-6000 Or 866-482-7488
VA Pittsburgh Healthcare System, Highland Drive Campus	7180 Highland Drive Pittsburgh, PA 15206	PA	412-360-6000 Or 866-482-7488
VA Pittsburgh Healthcare System, University Drive Campus	University Drive Pittsburgh, PA 15240	PA	412-360-6000 Or 866-482-7488
Wilkes-Barre VA Medical Center	1111 East End Blvd. Wilkes-Barre, PA 18711	PA	570-824-3521 Or 570-824-3521
VA Caribbean Healthcare System	10 Casia Street San Juan, PR 00921-3201	PR	787-641-7582 Or 787-641-7582
Providence VA Medical Center	830 Chalkstone Avenue Providence, RI 02908-4799	RI	401-273-7100 Or 866-363-4486
Ralph H. Johnson VA Medical Center	109 Bee Street Charleston, SC 29401-5799	SC	843-577-5011 Or 843-577-5011
Wm. Jennings Bryan Dorn VA Medical Center	6439 Garners Ferry Road Columbia, SC 29209-1639	SC	803-776-4000
Sioux Falls VA Health Care System	2501 W. 22nd Street, PO Box 5046 Sioux Falls, SD 57117-5046	SD	605-336-3230 Or 800-316-8387
VA Black Hills Health Care System - Hot Springs Campus	500 North 5th Street Hot Springs, SD 57747	SD	605-745-2000 Or 605-745-2000

VA Black Hills Health Care System - Fort Meade Campus	113 Comanche Road Fort Meade, SD 57741	SD	605-347-2511 Or 605-347-2511
Memphis VA Medical Center	1030 Jefferson Avenue Memphis, TN 38104	TN	901-523-8990 Or 901-523-8990
Mountain Home VAMC/Johnson City	Corner of Lamont Street and Veterans Way Mountain Home, TN 37684 Mailing Address: P.O. Box 4000 Mountain Home, TN 37684	TN	423-926-1171 Or 423-926-1171
Tennessee Valley Healthcare System	1310 24th Avenue South Nashville, TN 37212	TN	615-327-4751
Tennessee Valley Healthcare System - Alvin C. York (Murfreesboro) Campus	3400 Lebanon Pike Murfreesboro, TN 37129	TN	615-867-6000 Or 615-867-6000
Tennessee Valley Healthcare System - Nashville Campus	1310 24th Avenue South Nashville, TN 37212-2637	TN	615-327-4751 Or 615-327-4751
Amarillo VA Health Care System	6010 Amarillo Boulevard, West Amarillo, TX 79106	TX	806-355-9703 Or 806-355-9703
Central Texas Veterans Health Care System, Olin E. Teague Veterans Medical Center	1901 Veterans Memorial Drive Temple, TX 76504-7451	TX	254-778-4811 Or 254-778-4811
Dallas VA Medical Center	4500 S. Lancaster Rd. Dallas, TX 75216	TX	800-849-3597 Or 214-742-8387
El Paso VA Health Care System	5001 North Piedras Street El Paso, TX 79930-4211	TX	915-564-6100
Kerrville VA Hospital	3600 Memorial Blvd Kerrville, TX 78028	TX	830-896-2020 Or 866-487-7653
Michael E. DeBakey VA Medical Center	2002 Holcombe Blvd. Houston, TX 77030-4298	TX	713-791-1414 Or 713-791-1414
Sam Rayburn Memorial Veterans Center	1201 E. 9th St. Bonham, TX 75418	TX	800-924-8387 Or 800-924-8387
South Texas Veterans Health Care System	7400 Merton Minter Blvd. San Antonio, TX 78229	TX	210-617-5300 Or 210-617-5300
VA Health Care Center at Harlingen	2601 Veterans Drive Harlingen, TX 78550	TX	
VA North Texas Health Care System	4500 South Lancaster Road Dallas, TX 75216	TX	214-742-8387 Or 800-849-3597
VA Texas Valley Coastal Bend Health Care System	2601 Veterans Drive Harlingen, TX 78550	TX	956-291-9000
Waco VA Medical Center	4800 Memorial Drive Waco, TX 76711	TX	254-752-6581 Or 254-752-6581
West Texas VA Health Care System	300 Veterans Blvd. Big Spring, TX 79720	TX	432-263-7361 Or 432-263-7361
VA Salt Lake City Health Care System	500 Foothill Drive Salt Lake City, UT 84148	UT	801-582-1565
Hampton VA Medical Center	100 Emancipation Drive Hampton, VA 23667	VA	757-722-9961
Hunter Holmes McGuire VA Medical Center	1201 Broad Rock Boulevard Richmond, VA 23249	VA	804-675-5000
Salem VA Medical Center	1970 Roanoke Boulevard Salem, VA 24153	VA	540-982-2463 Or 888-982-2463
White River Junction VA Medical Center	163 Veterans Drive White River Junction, VT 05009 Mailing Address: 215 North Main Street White River Junction, VT 05009	VT	802-295-9363 Or 802-295-9363

Jonathan M. Wainwright Memorial VA Medical Center	77 Wainwright Drive Walla Walla, WA 99362	WA	888-687-8863 Or 888-687-8863
Mann-Grandstaff VA Medical Center	4815 N. Assembly Street Spokane, WA 99205	WA	509-434-7000
Portland VA Medical Center - Vancouver Campus	1601 E. 4th Plain Blvd Vancouver, WA 98661	WA	360-696-4061 Or 360-696-4061
VA Puget Sound Health Care System	1660 S. Columbian Way Seattle, WA 98108	WA	206-762-1010 Or 206-762-1010
VA Puget Sound Health Care System - American Lake Division	9600 Veterans Dr Lakewood, WA 98493	WA	253-582-8440 Or 253-582-8440
VA Puget Sound Health Care System - Seattle Division	1660 S. Columbian Way Seattle, WA 98108-1597	WA	206-762-1010 Or 800-329-8387
Clement J. Zablocki Veterans Affairs Medical Center	5000 West National Avenue Milwaukee, WI 53295-1000	WI	414-384-2000
Tomah VA Medical Center	500 E. Veterans Street Tomah, WI 54660	WI	608-372-3971
William S. Middleton Memorial Veterans Hospital	2500 Overlook Terrace Madison, WI 53705-2286	WI	608-256-1901 Or 608-256-1901
Beckley VA Medical Center	200 Veterans Avenue Beckley, WV 25801	WV	304-255-2121 Or 304-255-2121
Clarksburg - Louis A. Johnson VA Medical Center	One Medical Center Drive Clarksburg, WV 26301	WV	304-623-3461 Or 800-733-0512
Huntington VA Medical Center	1540 Spring Valley Drive Huntington, WV 25704	WV	304-429-6741
Martinsburg VA Medical Center	510 Butler Avenue Martinsburg, WV 25405	WV	304-263-0811 Or 800-817-3807
Cheyenne VA Medical	2360 E. Pershing Blvd. Cheyenne, WY 82001	WY	307-778-7550 Or 888-483-9127
Sheridan VA Medical Center	1898 Fort Road Sheridan, WY 82801	WY	307-672-3473 Or 307-672-3473

etnam Memorial at Angel Fire, NM

Authors at Vietnam Traveling Wall

Book Can Be Purchased At A
Volume Discount Through The Authors

Team Pursuits
c/o Tony & Jan Seahorn
3534 Harbor Way
Fort Collins, CO 80524
(970) 224-2425
tseahorn@att.net

www.tearsofawarrior.com

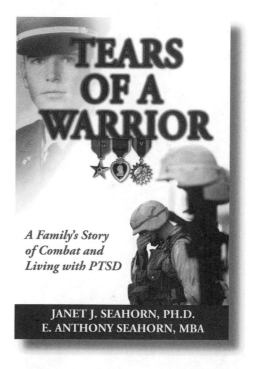

Note: The authors are also available for book signings, speaking engagements and seminars on the topic of PTSD

"The nation which forgets its defenders will itself be forgotten."

—Calvin Coolidge